CONTEN...

SYMBOLS

RESERVATIONS ACCEPTED	☎	JACKET AND TIE REQUIRED
FULL BAR	🍸	LIVE ENTERTAINMENT
VALET PARKING	🚗 PR	PRIVATE ROOM
VIEW	📷	OUTDOOR DINING
ROMANTIC	🍴	SPA CUISINE
LIVELY		NO SMOKING ANYWHERE

Lenox.

Because art is never an extravagance.

EPICUREAN RENDEZVOUS

PUBLISHER
Richard Brault

CO-PUBLISHER
Cynthia Turnbull

ASSOCIATE PUBLISHER
Chris Stauffenegger

EDITOR
Maia Madden

MANAGING EDITOR
Claudia Gioseffi

ASSOCIATE EDITOR
Mandy S. Page

ART DIRECTOR
Matthew Foster

COMPUTER GRAPHICS/DESIGN
Kat Cascone
John Farnsworth II

ASSISTANT TO THE ART DIRECTOR
Bob Hoffman

PRODUCTION ASSISTANTS
Patricia Fostar
Mimi Heft
Robin Bullard

PHOTOGRAPHY
Kingmond Young
Dawn Bryan   **Bruce Chin**

ADVERTISING DIRECTOR
Ana Gloria Pinto-Huson

ADVERTISING SERVICES MANAGER
Patricia Gregory

CIRCULATION DIRECTOR
Richard Moxley

CONTROLLER
Christine L. Megowan

ACCOUNTING DEPARTMENT
Djaja Hardjadinata
Harry Kurniawan

OFFICE ASSISTANT
Melanie Pauly

SAN FRANCISCO:
650 Fifth Street, #406, San Francisco, CA 94107
TEL: 415-777-2676 • FAX: 415-777-2637

NEW YORK:
75 Howell Avenue, Larchmont, NY 10538
TEL: 914-833-2676 • FAX: 914-833-0333

LOS ANGELES:
7466 Beverly Boulevard, #206, Los Angeles, CA 90036
TEL: 213-934-8656 • FAX: 213-934-9067

FLORIDA:
11426 Sundance Lane, Boca Raton, FL 33428
TEL: 407-451-2665 • FAX: 407-451-2884

EPICUREAN RENDEZVOUS

◆

"I have the simplest of tastes.
I am always satisfied with the best."

OSCAR WILDE

Epicurean Rendezvous is an annual guide to the best restaurants for those with the most discriminating tastes. An award program as well as a guide, *Epicurean Rendezvous* has four editions promoting the 100 finest restaurants in New York City, Los Angeles/Southern California, San Francisco/Northern California and Florida.

Restaurants do not pay to be included. They are selected by a local Advisory Board of volunteer critics, all food and wine experts. The criteria are simple:

1. The restaurant must serve consistently outstanding cuisine.
2. The staff must be courteous and knowledgeable and provide consistently excellent service.
3. The decor must be clean and attractive, and the ambiance, congenial.
4. The wine list must have the depth, breadth and balance to complement the cuisine.

Every year, the Advisory Board evaluates both new contenders and previous award-winners. Candidates are listed on a ballot, a vote is taken, and nominations are made. The publishers personally screen the finalists to determine the winners. Sometimes a restaurant will not meet every criterion but is so strong in one area that it deserves an award.

Once the Advisory Board selects its 100 award-winners, *Epicurean Rendezvous* leaves all critique behind. The only goal is to promote and elevate those who work hard to maintain the standards of fine dining. Sold on newsstands, the guides are also available in the restaurants, thereby creating a nationwide network of *Epicurean Rendezvous* diners.

Think of our reviews as short guided tours of each restaurant. They put you inside the dining room and introduce you to the owner or manager. You meet the chef, learn a little about his or her cooking style, and look over a sample menu. By the time you call for reservations, you'll feel confident that you've made the right choice.

THE ART OF FRENCH KISSING.

Pour two glasses of
Martell Cognac:
one for you and one
for someone you
love. Then proceed
to kiss in whatever
manner pleases you.

MARTELL

COGNAC. L'ART DE MARTELL.

SINCE 1715.

UNWIND

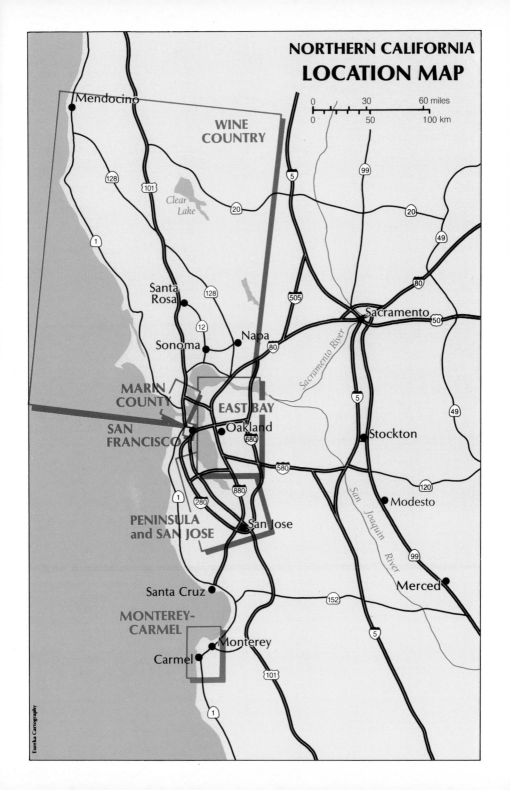

ABSOLUT
SAN FRANCISCO.

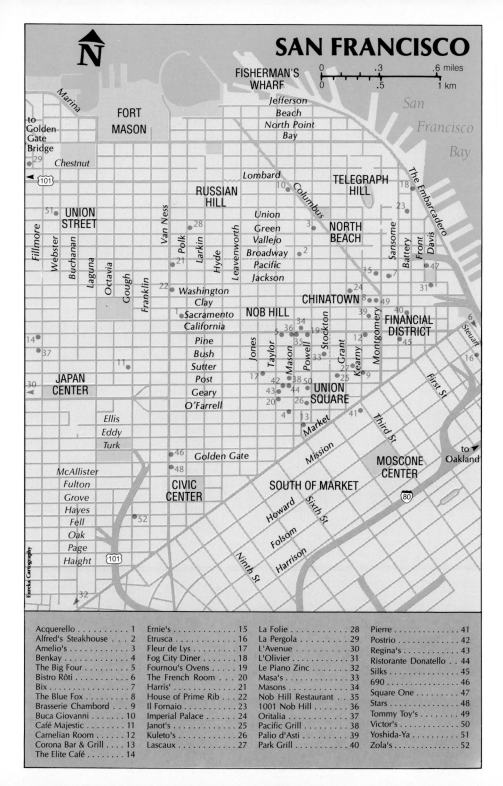

SAN FRANCISCO

N

FISHERMAN'S WHARF

0   .3   .6 miles
0   .5   1 km

Jefferson
Beach
North Point
Bay

FORT MASON

to Golden Gate Bridge

Chestnut

Marina

San Francisco Bay

RUSSIAN HILL

Lombard

Columbus

TELEGRAPH HILL

UNION STREET

Union
Green
Vallejo
Broadway
Pacific
Jackson

NORTH BEACH

Van Ness
Polk
Larkin
Hyde
Leavenworth

Fillmore
Webster
Buchanan
Laguna
Octavia
Gough
Franklin

Washington
Clay
Sacramento
California

NOB HILL

CHINATOWN

FINANCIAL DISTRICT

Sansome
Battery
Front
Davis

The Embarcadero

Stockton
Grant
Kearny
Montgomery

Pine
Bush
Sutter
Post
Geary
O'Farrell

Jones
Taylor
Mason
Powell

JAPAN CENTER

UNION SQUARE

Ellis
Eddy
Turk

Golden Gate

McAllister
Fulton
Grove
Hayes
Fell
Oak
Page
Haight

CIVIC CENTER

SOUTH OF MARKET

Market
Mission
Howard
Folsom
Harrison

Ninth St
Sixth St
First St
Third St
Stewart

MOSCONE CENTER

to Oakland

Eureka Cartography

SAMBUCA ROMANA

LIQUORE CLASSICO DI ROMA

ACQUERELLO

◆

1722 SACRAMENTO STREET
NEAR VAN NESS & POLK
SAN FRANCISCO, CA 94109
(415) 567-5432

MasterCard & Visa Only
Closed Monday • Dinner Only

Proprietor
GIANCARLO PATERLINI

Chef/Proprietor
SUZETTE GRESHAM

Menu Highlights

Appetizers
NEOPOLITAN SALAD OF
TOMATOES, MOZZARELLA,
ARUGULA & BLACK OLIVES
• PRAWNS IN BRANDY
WITH FRIED LEEKS •
HALF-MOON PASTA FILLED
WITH EGGPLANT & GOAT
CHEESE IN TOMATO SAUCE

Entrées
MARINATED LAMB LOIN
CHOPS WITH WHITE WINE,
GARLIC & ROSEMARY •
PORK LOIN ROLLED &
FILLED WITH PANCETTA,
RAISINS & PINE NUTS •
SPICY LOBSTER & PRAWN
FRICASSEE

ACQUERELLO MEANS WATERCOLOR IN ITALIAN, AND ENTER-ing the restaurant's dining room is like stepping into a painting. Pale pink walls dotted with soft lamps, a changing watercolor exhibit and pastel bouquets blend light and color, while clay tiles and rural beams provide contrast. ◆ Hailed as one of San Francisco's best Italian chefs when she was at Donatello, Suzette Gresham has a talent for rustic-style cooking, and her seasonal menu spans all regions of Italy. Proprietor Giancarlo Paterlini, a Bologna native who has earned a fine reputation in the restaurant business over the last nineteen years, met Gresham when he was the manager of Donatello. ◆ Uncovering lesser-known, interesting Italian and California vintages is Paterlini's passion, and offering them at a reasonable price is his forte. Once a month, Acquerello presents a special regional menu paired with the wines of a particular vintner, a rare opportunity to sample the talents of this inspired partnership.

AVERAGE DINNER FOR TWO: $70
DOES NOT INCLUDE WINE, TAX AND GRATUITY

ALFRED'S STEAKHOUSE

◆

886 BROADWAY
AT BROADWAY TUNNEL
SAN FRANCISCO, CA 94133
(415) 781-7058

Major Credit Cards
Open Daily for Dinner • Lunch Thursday Only

Proprietor
ART PETRI

Proprietor
AL PETRI

Menu Highlights

Appetizers
ESCARGOTS
BOURGUIGNONNE •
ITALIAN FRIED CALAMARI
• FRESH OYSTERS ON
THE HALF SHELL •
CAESAR SALAD • FRESH
ARTICHOKE

Entrées
ALFRED'S BONE-IN NEW
YORK STEAK •
CHATEAUBRIAND OF
BEEF TENDERLOIN,
SAUCE BÉARNAISE,
CARVED AT THE TABLE •
FILET MIGNON OF BEEF
TENDERLOIN • FRESH
SALMON, MESQUITE-
BROILED

SINCE 1928, ALFRED'S HAS SERVED ONLY THE FINEST PRIME cuts of juicy, corn-fed, skillfully aged steaks broiled over imported Mexican mesquite charcoal, producing tender, distinctively flavorful meat. Owner Al Petri recommends a tangy Caesar salad and an order of tortellini in a creamy pesto sauce as a start to dinner. ◆ At Alfred's, customers deliberate whether to order beef, veal, chicken or seafood and whether to have it mesquite-grilled or prepared in traditional Italian style (the cannelloni and fettuccini here are evidence of the North Beach-Italian tradition maintained at Alfred's). ◆ A thoroughly professional staff provides personal, attentive service in a rich clublike atmosphere that exudes Victorian luxury. Upstairs, banquet rooms can handle private parties of fifteen to fifty. Alfred's, offering the best of meat-and-potatoes Americana with an Italian touch, is an enduring San Francisco institution.

AVERAGE DINNER FOR TWO: $55
DOES NOT INCLUDE WINE, TAX AND GRATUITY

AMELIO'S

◆

1630 POWELL STREET
NEAR GREEN
SAN FRANCISCO, CA 94133
(415) 397-4339

Major Credit Cards
Closed Monday & Tuesday • Dinner Only

Proprietor
CHRIS SHEARMAN

Chef/Proprietor
JACKY ROBERT

Menu Highlights

Appetizers
BROILED MARINATED
PRAWNS • FRESH
FOIE GRAS SAUTÉED
WITH RASPBERRY
VINEGAR SAUCE •
WOVEN PASTA
WITH SHELLFISH

Entrées
ROASTED SQUAB
WITH STAR ANISE
SAUCE & WILD
RICE-SAFFRON
RISOTTO • SAUTÉED
YOUNG RABBIT
WITH GREENS &
POTATO PARASOL,
SESAME GLAZE

ESTABLISHED IN 1926, AMELIO'S, LONG A FAVORITE OF SAN Franciscans, catapulted into culinary leadership in 1985, when it won the services of one of the most widely respected and emulated chefs in the United States, Jacky Robert, who received the 1989 Association des Maîtres Cuisiniers de France award. Earlier in '89, the restaurant was given *The Wine Spectator* Grand Award. ◆ With fourteen tables downstairs and banquet facilities for up to sixty guests upstairs, proprietor Chris Shearman offers a choice of ambiance, from intimate to lively. A modest foyer belies the regal dining room just beyond the velvet curtain at Amelio's. Beautiful oil paintings and large mirrors in gilded frames enliven the dark wood-paneled walls. ◆ Amelio's is not the place for a quick, pre-theatre meal; the meticulously prepared menus are meant to be savored. As co-owner, Chef Robert has complete creative freedom, and his genius is blossoming. Amelio's menus showcase his unique presentation and finesse.

AVERAGE DINNER FOR TWO: $80
DOES NOT INCLUDE WINE, TAX AND GRATUITY

BENKAY

◆

HOTEL NIKKO
222 MASON STREET
SAN FRANCISCO, CA 94102
(415) 394-1105

Major Credit Cards
Open Daily for Dinner • Breakfast & Lunch Mon-Fri

Director
S. FUJIMOTO

Chef
N. MIYAGAWA

Menu Highlights

Dinners
CALIFORNIA KAISEKI:
WESTERN FAVORITES
INCLUDING APPETIZERS,
GRILLED SELECTIONS,
TEMPURA, FRESH BROTH,
SASHIMI, SUSHI, RICE &
MISO SOUP • TOKIWA
KAISEKI: DELUXE
TEN-COURSE DINNER OF
FISH, FOWL, MEAT &
VEGETABLES • TEMPURA
KAISEKI: APPETIZERS,
SASHIMI, SIMMERED
VEGETABLES, PRAWN, FISH
& VEGETABLE TEMPURA,
SALAD, RICE, MISO SOUP
& DESSERT

STEPPING OFF THE ELEVATOR ON THE TWENTY-FIFTH FLOOR of the Hotel Nikko, you enter a world so serene that stress falls away with each step across the silver-gray carpet. With its intimate waiting areas, meditational rock gardens and large windows framing the city's skyline, Benkay is a beautiful setting for Kaiseki, a cuisine derived from the Japanese tea ceremony. ◆ Unfamiliar even to some Japanese, Kaiseki consists of a succession of many exquisite courses composed to harmonize taste, color and texture. The service by kimono-clad waitresses obeys tradition, as does the presentation on imported porcelain and lacquer dishes, each specific to a course. ◆ In addition to Kaiseki, Benkay offers a menu of à la carte dishes in its sleek, contemporary dining room. To experience the full pleasure of Kaiseki, reserve one of Benkay's six private tatami rooms.

AVERAGE DINNER FOR TWO: $90
DOES NOT INCLUDE WINE, TAX AND GRATUITY

THE BIG FOUR

◆

HUNTINGTON HOTEL
1075 CALIFORNIA STREET
SAN FRANCISCO, CA 94108
(415) 771-1140

Major Credit Cards
Open Daily • Breakfast, Lunch & Dinner

Manager
NEWTON A. COPE, JR.

Chef
GLORIA CICCARONE

Menu Highlights

Appetizers
ITALIAN EGG SOUP
WITH GARLIC
CROUTONS &
PANCETTA • SMOKED
LAMB CARPACCIO WITH
MINT & TOASTED
PUMPKIN SEEDS

Entrées
TEA-SMOKED PEKING
DUCK WITH MANGO &
SHRIMP WONTONS •
PINE NUT-COATED
ROASTED VEAL CHOP
WITH BASIL,
MOZZARELLA &
TOMATO CREAM

ALL HIS LIFE, NEWTON A. COPE, SR., WAS CAPTIVATED BY THE colorful history of the "Big Four": C.P. Huntington, Charles Crocker, Mark Hopkins and Leland Stanford, railroad men who built their empires after 1869 and became San Francisco's wealthiest, most influential citizens. Thirteen years ago, he opened The Big Four in the Huntington Hotel and filled the restaurant with his extensive collection of California art, Big Four political cartoons, railroad prints and other historical memorabilia. ♦ Restaurant manager Newton A. Cope, Jr., has strived to establish a culinary reputation for The Big Four equal to the old-world traditions championed by his father. ♦ With the help of Chef Gloria Ciccarone, that reputation is assured. "We are receptive to innovation, especially with our daily specials," she says, "but we pride ourselves on serving local ingredients and a menu that changes with the seasons."

AVERAGE DINNER FOR TWO: $60
DOES NOT INCLUDE WINE, TAX AND GRATUITY

BISTRO ROTI
◆

HOTEL GRIFFON
155 STEUART STREET
SAN FRANCISCO, CA 94105
(415) 495-6500

Major Credit Cards
Dinner Daily • Lunch Mon-Fri • Sat & Sun Brunch

Manager
DAVID O'MALLEY

Chef
ROBERT CUBBERLY

Menu Highlights

Appetizers
CRISP SWEETBREADS
WITH LEMONS, LEEKS
& CAPERS • WARM
CHICORY FRISÉE
WITH APPLE-SMOKED
BACON & GOAT
CHEESE • FRENCH
ONION SOUP

Entrées
ROASTED CHICKEN
BREAST "COQ AU VIN"
STYLE • SPIT-ROASTED
DUCK WITH PICKLED
FIG CHUTNEY •
GRILLED VEAL CHOP
WITH HERBS OF
PROVENCE

ONCE AN OLD SEAMEN'S HAUNT, BISTRO ROTI IN THE HOTEL Griffon is now a dynamic gathering place for the downtown crowd. Guests enter a book-lined marble foyer, then pass through a cozy bistro area with French-style zinc bar. A rustic open rotisserie gives way to a leather- and brass-appointed dining room, followed by a mezzanine dining room with a gleaming open kitchen and a view of the waterfront. ◆ In this warm, richly textured setting, Chef Robert Cubberly takes Rôti's French-inspired American cuisine to glorious heights. Formerly at the Four Seasons Clift and Fog City Diner, the Seattle native combines Northern California produce, fresh local seafood, and spit-roasted fowl, meats and game in a hearty, bistro-style menu lightened to suit American tastes. "Potatoes 3rd Arrondissement" and seasoned onion rings are musts with any entrée. ◆ Rôti's collection of French and California wines focuses on mellow reds — Merlots, Rhônes and Syrahs — and rich whites — Sancerres and Sauvignon Blancs.

AVERAGE DINNER FOR TWO: $60
DOES NOT INCLUDE WINE, TAX AND GRATUITY

REMY MARTIN est l'eau de vie

COGNAC XO SPECIAL
EXCLUSIVEMENT FINE CHAMPAGNE COGNAC
DEPUIS 1724

BOMBAY SAPPHIRE.
POUR SOMETHING PRICELESS

BIX

56 GOLD STREET
AT MONTGOMERY
SAN FRANCISCO, CA 94133
(415) 433-6300
Major Credit Cards
Open Daily for Dinner • Lunch Mon-Fri

Proprietor
DOUG BIEDERBECK

Chef
GORDON DRYSDALE

Menu Highlights

Appetizers
SWEET CORN CUSTARD •
SONOMA FOIE GRAS WITH
ARTICHOKE HEART •
WALDORF SALAD WITH
BLUE CHEESE • STEAK
TARTARE • POTATO &
LEEK PANCAKE WITH
SMOKED SALMON &
CAVIAR

Entrées
PORK CHOP WITH MASHED
POTATOES & GARDEN PEAS
• ROASTED RACK OF LAMB
PERSILLÉ • ROASTED
DUCK BREAST WITH
POLENTA & RED CABBAGE
• PAN-FRIED CHICKEN

TO REACH ONE OF SAN FRANCISCO'S LIVELIEST RESTAURANTS, go down a quiet alley off Montgomery Street near Jackson Square to a plain brick building flanked by antique galleries. Inside is Bix, a tribute to the Jazz Age and Art Moderne that Doug ("Bix") Biederbeck calls "an updated supper club," complete with torch singer, saxophone player and pianist. ◆ Bix recalls the era of the majestic ocean liner, with curving Honduras mahogany, silver columns and reproductions of late 1920s ceiling lamps. A huge, deep-hued mural of a jazz club scene is the focal point. Underneath, behind the always-jammed bar, white-jacketed bartenders ring in the renaissance of the cocktail with deftly prepared Manhattans, Sidecars and Martinis. ◆ The menu is filled with offerings that sound simple and straightforward. Modern culinary flourishes jazz up each one, to surprise and delight the palate.

AVERAGE DINNER FOR TWO: $50
DOES NOT INCLUDE WINE, TAX AND GRATUITY

21

THE BLUE FOX

◆

659 MERCHANT STREET
AT MONTGOMERY
SAN FRANCISCO, CA 94111
(415) 981-1177

Major Credit Cards
Closed Sunday • Dinner Only

Proprietor
GIANNI FASSIO

Chef
PATRIZIO SACCHETTO

Menu Highlights

Appetizers
VENISON CARPACCIO WITH
ESSENCE OF WHITE
TRUFFLE • LOBSTER TAIL
WITH SAFFRON • RAINBOW
PAPPARDELLE, BASIL
BUTTER SAUCE • RISOTTO
WITH WHITE TRUFFLES

Entrées
STEAMED HALIBUT,
EGGPLANT SAUCE •
GRILLED VEAL CHOP WITH
PORCINI MUSHROOMS •
ROASTED PHEASANT WITH
YELLOW BELL PEPPER
COULIS • ROASTED BREAST
OF MUSCOVY DUCK WITH
FOIE GRAS SAUCE

AS A TEENAGER, GIANNI FASSIO WORKED IN HIS FATHER'S restaurant, The Blue Fox, and for years he dreamed of someday making it his own. When he finally bought it three years ago, Fassio left a successful career as an international C.P.A. to transform The Blue Fox into one of San Francisco's top Italian restaurants. ◆ Chef Patrizio Sacchetto, formerly of Rex, Il Ristorante in Los Angeles and a teacher at the California Culinary Academy, recreates the aristocratic cuisine of sixteenth- and seventeenth-century Italy. His adept balance of richness and freshness, tradition and innovation, has earned high praise. ◆ The Blue Fox's impeccable service has been maintained, as has its large wine cellar, but with a new emphasis on Italian wines. The elegant, formal dining room is softened by mirrors, peach-toned walls and comfortable upholstered chairs. The two legendary private rooms, where generations of San Franciscans have celebrated special occasions, are again in constant demand.

AVERAGE DINNER FOR TWO: $90
DOES NOT INCLUDE WINE, TAX AND GRATUITY

BRASSERIE CHAMBORD

◆

152 KEARNY STREET
AT SUTTER
SAN FRANCISCO, CA 94104
(415) 434-3688

Major Credit Cards
Closed Sunday • Breakfast, Lunch & Dinner

Proprietors	*Chef*
JEAN-CLAUDE LAIR	ALEX J. ERRECARTE
GIORGIO ALLEGRO	

Menu Highlights

Appetizers
FRESH TERRINE OF FOIE GRAS • ESCARGOTS BOURGUIGNONNE • SMOKED STURGEON WITH HORSERADISH & SOUR CREAM

Entrées
DUCK CONFIT • BARBECUED CHICKEN SALAD • GRILLED LAMB CHOPS WITH ROSEMARY SAUCE • POACHED COLD SALMON • BABY LOBSTER WRAPPED IN BACON WITH TARRAGON SAUCE • GRILLED WARM TUNA WITH FRESH TOMATO & HERBS

MIDWAY BETWEEN SAN FRANCISCO'S FINANCIAL DISTRICT and the shopping mecca of Union Square, a Frenchman and a Venetian have created an authentic, lively brasserie. ◆ Owners Jean-Claude Lair and Giorgio Allegro opened this unique establishment in 1982. Either of them can be found cutting fresh flowers, restocking the wine racks, inspecting the daily produce deliveries or looking over the skillfully presented plates leaving the kitchen. Such vigilantly maintained high standards keep a staunchly loyal clientele coming back. ◆ "I love to research the traditional French recipes," says Chef Alex Errecarte, who is Basque in heritage, "and discover an over-looked herb or nuance that can give my customers more pleasure from my cooking." ◆ He changes his French regional specialties every two weeks and has recently added a new spa menu. A chalkboard lists French and California wines available by the glass.

AVERAGE DINNER FOR TWO: $40
DOES NOT INCLUDE WINE, TAX AND GRATUITY

BUCA GIOVANNI

◆

800 GREENWICH STREET
NEAR COLUMBUS
SAN FRANCISCO, CA 94133
(415) 776-7766

Major Credit Cards
Closed Sunday • Dinner Only

Chef/Proprietor
GIOVANNI LEONI

Chef/Proprietor
DAVID SIERING

Menu Highlights

Appetizers
WARM RABBIT SALAD
WITH RADICCHIO •
ANTIPASTO MISTO LA
BUCA • ROUND RAVIOLINI
STUFFED WITH EGGPLANT
& GORGONZOLA IN A
BASIL SAUCE
Entrées
RABBIT WITH GRAPPA •
VENISON WITH WILD
FENNEL • ROASTED
SCAMPI WRAPPED IN
PROSCIUTTO • LAMB
STUFFED WITH
MORTADELLA, HERBS &
PORCINI MUSHROOMS
& WRAPPED IN
GRAPE LEAVES

TRUE TO ITS NAME, GIOVANNI'S "CAVE" IS A ROMANTIC BRICK-walled retreat down a short flight of stairs. The real action, however, is in the open kitchen upstairs, where those seated at the few small tables can watch Giovanni Leoni and his partner, David Siering, prepare their Tuscan specialties. ◆ Leoni, who was chef at Vanessi's for eighteen years before opening his restaurant seven years ago, directs every aspect of Buca Giovanni. Up at dawn, he does the daily marketing, and on Sundays, returns from a visit to his family ranch in Ukiah with dozens of rabbits in the back of his car. Leoni grows his own herbs, lettuce and tomatoes, and will search for years to find the best ricotta and the finest coffee beans, which he then roasts himself on the premises. ◆ His exacting standards can be tasted in every preparation, from the earthy *salsa rosa*, an addictive purée of sundried tomatoes, anchovies, garlic, capers and vinegar, to the ethereal ricotta gnocchi.

AVERAGE DINNER FOR TWO: $50
DOES NOT INCLUDE WINE, TAX AND GRATUITY

CAFÉ MAJESTIC

THE HOTEL MAJESTIC
1500 SUTTER STREET
SAN FRANCISCO, CA 94109
(415) 776-6400

Major Credit Cards
Open Daily • Breakfast, Lunch & Dinner

Proprietors
TOM MARSHALL
ROLF LEWIS

Chef
PETER DEMARAIS

Menu Highlights

Appetizers
WARM QUAIL SALAD
YERBA BUENA ON
LIMESTONE LETTUCE WITH
RUBY GRAPEFRUIT &
MINT-SHERRY
VINAIGRETTE • LOBSTER
& SCALLOP RAVIOLI,
SAUCE AMÉRICAINE

Entrées
RACK OF LAMB MAISON
D'OR WITH PARMESAN &
HORSERADISH • GRILLED
VEAL CHOP WITH FRESH
SAGE & MELTED BLEU
D'AUVERGNE

OWNER TOM MARSHALL HAS CREATED A RESTAURANT THAT embodies the best of San Francisco, balancing Victorian grandeur with contemporary vitality. Situated off the lobby of the Hotel Majestic, Café Majestic has a stunning dining room lovingly restored from 1907 photographs of the original. Light and airy during the day, it becomes elegantly romantic at night. Adjoining the restaurant is a beautiful 125-year-old bar, imported from a café in Paris. ◆ To complement the turn-of-the-century decor, Chef Peter DeMarais interprets recipes from early San Francisco restaurants, giving them a modern twist. A perfect example is his Chicken Nellie Melba, grilled and topped with lychee nuts in a wild mushroom sauce.

AVERAGE DINNER FOR TWO: $60
DOES NOT INCLUDE WINE, TAX AND GRATUITY

CARNELIAN ROOM

BANK OF AMERICA BUILDING
555 CALIFORNIA STREET
SAN FRANCISCO, CA 94104
(415) 433-7500

Major Credit Cards
Open Daily for Dinner • Sunday Brunch

General Manager
JOHN NELSON

Chef
GABRIEL ELICETCHE

Menu Highlights

Appetizers
TIMBALE OF SMOKED
SALMON FILLED WITH
SMOKED TROUT MOUSSE •
POACHED TIGER PRAWNS
WITH LOBSTER MOUSSE

Entrées
PACIFIC ABALONE
SAUTÉED WITH SCALLIONS,
LEMON & PEPPER SAUCE •
FRESH LINGUINI TOSSED
WITH SAUTÉED ROCK
SHRIMP • SAUTÉED
PETALUMA DUCK BREAST
AND CONFIT OF LEG WITH
LENTILS, GINGER &
PEPPER SAUCE

SOARING FIFTY-TWO STORIES ABOVE SAN FRANCISCO'S Financial District, the Carnelian Room offers a panoramic view of the Bay Area. The Bank of America's polished granite building is a fitting home for this elegant dining establishment. ◆General Manager John Nelson has guided the restaurant on its course of excellence since it opened nineteen years ago. Chef Gabriel Elicetche, trained in France's Basque country, changes his menu twice yearly and his specials every day to fully utilize California's rich variety of vegetables, fruit, seafood, fowl, beef and game. ◆ By day, the Carnelian Room is the exclusive Banker's Club, accessible only to members or by invitation. The restaurant is open to the public at night and for Sunday brunch, banquets and catered events. ◆The Carnelian Room's extensive wine list, recipient of *The Wine Spectator* Grand Award, features a cellar of 36,000 bottles.

AVERAGE DINNER FOR TWO: $75
DOES NOT INCLUDE WINE, TAX AND GRATUITY

WHITE RABBITS,
MOSCOW AND POLISH VODKA.

NICE TOWN, MOSCOW. RED SQUARE, ANCIENT SPIRES, FUR HATS, CAPITALISTS... AND A VERITABLE MONOPOLY ON THE WORLD'S GREAT VODKAS. WHICH BRINGS US TO AN INTERESTING PIECE OF TRIVIA ABOUT WHAT IS ARGUABLY THE FINEST VODKA IN ALL OF RUSSIA. WYBOROWA (VEE-BA-ROVA). IT ISN'T RUSSIAN. IT'S POLISH VODKA.

FIRST DISTILLED CENTURIES AGO. AND LEGENDARY EVER SINCE.

SO LEGENDARY THAT THE RUSSIANS DID WHAT ANY COUNTRY OF 140,000,000 VODKA FANATICS WOULD DO. THEY IMPORTED IT. BUT THEN, WYBOROWA HAS ALWAYS HAD A SLIGHTLY ECCENTRIC HISTORY. THERE WERE ALWAYS, FOR INSTANCE, RACCOONS, LAYING HENS AND WHITE POLISH RABBITS ON THE GROUNDS OF ITS DISTILLERY. WHY HAS WYBOROWA SURVIVED FOR CENTURIES? TASTE IT. YOU'LL FIND IT INEFFABLY SMOOTH. CRISP. A RESULT OF THE SAME TRIPLE-DISTILLING PROCESS USED CENTURIES AGO. BEFORE THEY DISCOVERED SHORTCUTS. TODAY, IT IS POSSIBLE TO ENJOY WYBOROWA RIGHT HERE IN AMERICA. WHAT BETTER WAY TO TOAST THE END OF THE COLD WAR.

"VEE-BA-ROVA" VODKA FROM POLAND. ENJOYED FOR CENTURIES STRAIGHT.

CORONA BAR & GRILL

◆

MONTICELLO INN
88 CYRIL MAGNIN STREET
SAN FRANCISCO, CA 94102
(415) 392-5500

Major Credit Cards
Open Daily for Dinner • Lunch Mon-Sat

Manager
MARK STAMLER

Chef
REED HEARON

Menu Highlights

Appetizers
PORCINI MUSHROOM
QUESADILLA WITH
ROASTED CORN &
SUNDRIED TOMATO
SALSA • LAMB BIRRIA
SOPES (CORN MASA
TARTLETS) WITH
PAPAYA SALAD &
SALSA RANCHERO

Entrées
PAELLA VALENCIANA
WITH PRAWNS,
CLAMS, MUSSELS,
CHICKEN & SAFFRON •
TUNA CAMPECHE
LAYERED ON
CORN TORTILLAS

THE CORONA BAR & GRILL IS NOT YOUR TYPICAL MEXICAN restaurant, thanks to Chef Reed Hearon. A thirteen-year restaurant veteran who helped open Mark Miller's Coyote Café in Santa Fe and Rattlesnake Club in Denver, he relies on ultra-fresh ingredients, intense flavors and no cream or butter in his free-reined interpretations of regional Mexican cuisine. Unique and sometimes startling, his combinations appeal to the creative palate. ◆ A festive yet relaxed mood prevails at the Corona, much like that of Mexico itself, making it popular with theatre-goers, shoppers, local businessmen and journalists. Designed by Pat Kuleto to resemble a Mexican sunset, Corona's decor of copper and verdigris is accented by Southwestern motifs and united by a ninety-foot cherrywood bar adorned with authentic totem masks. Here, one can enjoy everything from appetizers to a full meal. ◆ Corona's excellent margaritas are reputed to be the best in town, but oenophiles will appreciate the wine list, carefully chosen to complement the piquant dishes.

AVERAGE DINNER FOR TWO: $40
DOES NOT INCLUDE WINE, TAX AND GRATUITY

THE ELITE CAFÉ

◆

2049 FILLMORE STREET
AT CALIFORNIA
SAN FRANCISCO, CA 94115
(415) 346-8668

Major Credit Cards
Open Daily for Dinner • Sunday Brunch

Proprietor
TOM CLENDENING

Chef
SCOTT GMAZEL

Menu Highlights

Appetizers
OYSTERS IN
HELL • CREOLE
GUMBO • SHRIMP
REMOULADE • FRESH
LOUISIANA CRAWFISH •
SELECT OYSTERS

Entrées
LOUISIANA CHAURICE
SAUSAGE WITH RED
BEANS & RICE •
STUFFED CREOLE
EGGPLANT •
CRABCAKES •
BARBECUED BABY BACK
RIBS • BLACKENED
PORK LOUISIANA

ANY NIGHT OF THE WEEK, A STYLISH CROWD PACKS THE BAR
at The Elite Café, one of the more popular, vibrant dining spots in San
Francisco. Dark polished wood trim runs the length of the dining
room, adding to The Elite's New Orleans fishhouse atmosphere, and
a lively crowd mingles at the oyster bar. For quiet dining, several private booths are set along the walls. ◆ The original Creole restaurant on
the West Coast, The Elite helped popularize this American regional
cuisine. Chef Scott Gmazel uses cast-iron pans to prepare blackened
redfish fresh from the Pacific and blackened filet mignon. The soft-
shell crabs, flown in from Chesapeake Bay, are a specialty, and the
desserts are not to be missed. ◆ Proprietor Tom Clendening has created a signature restaurant that's both friendly and reliable. The wine
list specializes in California bottlings with an emphasis on white wines.

AVERAGE DINNER FOR TWO: $40
DOES NOT INCLUDE WINE, TAX AND GRATUITY

ERNIE'S

◆

847 MONTGOMERY STREET
AT PACIFIC
SAN FRANCISCO, CA 94133
(415) 397-5969

Major Credit Cards
Open Daily • Dinner Only

Proprietors
VICTOR GOTTI
ROLAND GOTTI

Chef
ALAIN RONDELLI

Menu Highlights

Appetizers
LEEK SALAD WITH OSETRA
CAVIAR & LEMON CREAM •
SMOKED SALMON TART
WITH ASPARAGUS, BLACK
OLIVES, TOMATO & FRESH
HERB SALAD
Entrées
ROASTED DUCK IN TWO
COURSES: BREAST SERVED
WITH ITS OWN JUICE &
GREENS, & LEGS EN
CONFIT IN CORN CUSTARD
WITH SHERRY SAUCE •
PAN-ROASTED VEAL
CHOP WITH MARINATED
OLIVES & CONFIT
OF TOMATO

IN A CITY OF RESTAURANT LEGENDS, ERNIE'S REIGNS SUPREME.
What began in 1934 as a small Italian eatery with linoleum floors and
modestly set tables has grown into a showplace of elegant decor and
French cuisine using the freshest California ingredients. ◆ The recent
arrival from France of gifted Chef Alain Rondelli, hailed for his expertise in the kitchens of Michelin three-star L'Esperance in Saint Père
sous Vezelay, and Mas de Chastelas in St. Tropez, has infused the
menu with the best of France's current food trends. "Modern French
cuisine is very simple," says the 29-year-old Rondelli. "Fewer ingredients are combined well to heighten rather than mask the natural flavors of the ingredients." ◆ The Bacchus Wine Cellar, available for private parties, houses a wine selection recognized as one of America's
finest and honored by *The Wine Spectator* Grand Award since its
inception. Ernie's was also a recipient of Mobil's Five Star Award for
twenty-seven consecutive years — an American record.

AVERAGE DINNER FOR TWO: $90
DOES NOT INCLUDE WINE, TAX AND GRATUITY

ETRUSCA

RINCON CENTER
121 SPEAR STREET
SAN FRANCISCO, CA 94111
(415) 777-0330

MasterCard & Visa Only
Open Daily • Lunch & Dinner

Managing Partner
UMBERTO GIBIN

Chef
RUGGERO GATALDI

Menu Highlights

Appetizers
TIMBALE OF GRILLED
EGGPLANT, ARTICHOKE &
SPINACH ON BELL PEPPER
PURÉE • PASTA TUBES &
DUCK RAGU BÉCHAMEL
SAUCE WITH PARMESAN,
BAKED IN THE WOOD-
BURNING OVEN

Entrées
RACK OF LAMB
STUFFED WITH FETA
CHEESE & FRESH MINT
ON BLACK OLIVE SAUCE •
GRILLED HALF CHICKEN
WITH KALAMATA OLIVES,
BELL PEPPERS,
SAGE & LEMON

FOR THEIR LATEST SUCCESS, LARRY MINDEL, CREATOR OF IL Fornaio, and managing partner Umberto Gibin have reinterpreted the cuisine of the ancient Etruscans. After a trip to Italy to retrace the steps of these highly cultured people, they built a menu with a Tuscan soul and an Adriatic heart. Based on meat, game, fish and pasta, its rich, smoky flavors come from a magnificent Etruscan-style oven visible from the dining room. There's even an Etruscan pizza: feta, arugula, goat cheese and sundried tomatoes on a semolina crust. ◆A golden glow permeates Etrusca, the result of bird's-eye maple walls stained a deep butterscotch. Sunny by day, the light turns flattering and romantic at night. On the ceilings, frescoes copied from Etruscan tomb paintings depict festive banquets. Cozy booths provide comfort and privacy. ◆For more action, a lively bar overlooks the dining room, with a special menu served until midnight on weekends, fifteen wines by the glass, more than 180 grappas and an extensive selection of single malt scotches.

AVERAGE DINNER FOR TWO: $60
DOES NOT INCLUDE WINE, TAX AND GRATUITY

FLEUR DE LYS

◆

777 SUTTER STREET
NEAR JONES
SAN FRANCISCO, CA 94109
(415) 673-7779

Major Credit Cards
Closed Sunday • Dinner Only

Proprietor
MAURICE ROUAS

Chef/Proprietor
HUBERT KELLER

Menu Highlights

Appetizers

MAINE LOBSTER WITH
FLAGEOLETS & BLACK
CHANTERELLES IN A
CILANTRO BROTH •
AMERICAN FOIE GRAS
TERRINE IN A BLACK
PEPPER & FRESH
HERB GELEE

Entrées

BROILED STRIPED BASS ON
A BED OF CHOUCROUTE
WITH A JUNIPER BERRY &
RED WINE SAUCE • VEAL
LOIN ROLLED OVER
TOASTED TRI-COLOR BELL
PEPPERS & SWEET ONIONS
WITH A SHALLOT
THYME SAUCE

EVEN THOUGH FLEUR DE LYS HAS HAD A DEVOTED CLIEN-
tele since it opened in 1970, in 1986 Maurice Rouas decided to give
his restaurant a shot in the arm. He did what many others before him
had tried without success: he lured the talented Hubert Keller to
Fleur de Lys as his new partner and chef. ◆ Educated at the Hotel
School in Strasbourg, France, Keller trained under such legendary
chefs as Paul Haeberlin, Paul Bocuse, Gaston Lenôtre and Roger
Vergé. "I believe," he says, "in the sweetness of the onion, the green
of the striped tigerella, the subtlety of the leek, the pervasiveness of
the garlic and the intensity of Florence fennel." ◆ The dramatic setting
of Fleur de Lys suits Keller's award-winning cuisine, which, although
steeped in classical tradition, welcomes the challenge of California's
culinary revolution. Designed by the late Michael Taylor, the dining
room is draped with hundreds of yards of hand-painted red floral fabric, like an immense garden tent.

AVERAGE DINNER FOR TWO: $100
DOES NOT INCLUDE WINE, TAX AND GRATUITY

FOG CITY DINER

◆

1300 BATTERY STREET
AT EMBARCADERO
SAN FRANCISCO, CA 94133
(415) 982-2000

Mastercard & Visa Only
Open Daily • Lunch & Dinner

Proprietor
BILL HIGGINS

Chef/Proprietor
CINDY PAWLCYN

Menu Highlights

Appetizers
CRABCAKES WITH SHERRY-CAYENNE MAYONNAISE • GARLIC CUSTARD WITH MUSHROOMS, CHIVES & CHOPPED SEASONED WALNUTS • GRILLED STUFFED PASILLA PEPPER WITH AVOCADO SALSA

Entrées
SEVERAL SALADS ON A PLATE • GRILLED SKIRT STEAK WITH TOMATO AIOLI • DINER CHILI DOG • PORK CHOPS WITH HOUSEMADE GINGER APPLESAUCE & GLAZED CARROTS

AS A CHILD IN CHICAGO, SAYS BILL HIGGINS, "THE DINER WAS the first restaurant I understood. The food was accessible, and I liked being able to watch the cooks." When Higgins grew up, he opened his very own diner, with updated diner food and such adult touches as a full bar and a sexy, streamlined interior. ◆ With its chrome and neon facade, Fog City Diner is a trendsetter, one of the first restaurants to encourage patrons to sample its specialties by sharing a variety of appetizers. Cindy Pawlcyn's menu centers around "small plates" made for "grazing," a practice now popular in restaurants around the country. ◆ If you prefer traditional diner fare, you won't be disappointed. The menu is full of middle-American favorites like milkshakes and chili dogs, made modern but not nouvelle. Fog City's success has spawned lots of neo-diners imitating its inspired menu and sleek decor. But don't be fooled — there's no topping the original.

AVERAGE DINNER FOR TWO: $45
DOES NOT INCLUDE WINE, TAX AND GRATUITY

TABBAH. FOR THOSE WHO KNOW

COLLECTION BLUE BERET

Tabbah

MYTHOLOGY

If you've been drinking a fine blended scotch like Chivas, Black Label, or Pinch, the idea that there's something even smoother, something even more distinctive, sounds like pure fantasy.

REALITY

But there is something smoother. Something more distinctive. Glenfiddich. The pure malt scotch that isn't blended with grain whiskies. Just try it once. And you'll find mythology is reality.

FOURNOU'S OVENS

◆

STANFORD COURT • A STOUFFER HOTEL
905 CALIFORNIA STREET
SAN FRANCISCO, CA 94108
(415) 989-1910

Major Credit Cards
Open Daily • Dinner Only

Food & Beverage Director
YVES BHERENS

Executive Chef
LAWRENCE VITO

Menu Highlights

Appetizers
GRILLED SHIITAKE
MUSHROOMS MARINATED
IN OLIVE OIL
& BALSAMIC VINEGAR

Entrées
OAK-ROASTED RACK
OF LAMB WITH
CORN & POZOLE
CUSTARD IN
ANCHO CHILE
& ROASTED PEPPER
SAUCE • SMOKED
BRADLEY RANCH
RIB EYE WITH
POTATO SPIRALS &
ANCHOR STEAM
BEER SAUCE

FIRED WITH OAK LOGS, THE SEVEN VAST OVENS AT Fournou's are modeled after the 267-year-old ovens of Casa Botin, one of the oldest restaurants in Madrid. Now owned by Stouffer and under the direction of Executive Chef Lawrence Vito, Fournou's Ovens presents house specialties such as rack of lamb, beef, veal and game roasted to perfection. A blend of fresh herbs, olive oil and exotic marinades enhances the full flavors of naturally raised meats, poultry and seafood, and organically grown produce emphasizes the chef's respect for healthful eating. ◆ The Mediterranean tenor of the restaurant's lower level is created by fine antiques, paintings from Europe, and copper-roofed terraces reminiscent of the glass-enclosed winter gardens of the nineteenth century. Just a few steps beyond the interior greenery, cable cars cascade down Nob Hill. ◆ Cellar Master Peter Granoff maintains the restaurant's impeccable standards with a wine cellar that houses 21,000 bottles and contains one of the nation's largest selections of California wines.

AVERAGE DINNER FOR TWO: $80
DOES NOT INCLUDE WINE, TAX AND GRATUITY

THE FRENCH ROOM

◆

FOUR SEASONS CLIFT HOTEL
495 GEARY STREET
SAN FRANCISCO, CA 94102
(415) 775-4700

Major Credit Cards
Open Daily • Breakfast, Lunch & Dinner • Sunday Brunch

Maitre d'
HEINZ EGGER

Chef
KELLY MILLS

Menu Highlights

Appetizers
CAPPELLINI & ZUCCHINI,
WITH SUMMER TOMATO
COULIS • PRAWN TEMPURA
WITH BLACK SESAME
STICKY RICE, DAIKON
ROOT & PLUM SAUCE

Entrées
GRILLED AHI TUNA, WITH
WHITE CORN & GOAT
CHEESE TAMALE •
GRILLED LAMB CHOP,
WITH OVEN-DRIED
TOMATO & PEPPERS
RELLENOS À LA GRECQUE
• GINGER-BLACK-PEPPER-
CRUSTED SALMON, WITH
LOBSTER POTSTICKERS

NOTHING CAN DUPLICATE THE PAMPERED FEELING OF DIN-ing in the historic, high-ceilinged splendor of The French Room or sipping a drink in the majestic Redwood Room at a bar made of one solid redwood burl. Its 1934 outlines meticulously preserved, The French Room upholds its standing as a city favorite for power break-fasts, elegant luncheons and very romantic dinners. ◆While faithful to its tradition of impeccable formal service, The French Room is con-stantly innovating. One of the first chefs to lighten the French classics and insist on fresh, locally grown produce and naturally raised meats, Kelly Mills has also shown the way with his "alternative cuisine," selections low in calories, fat and sodium. He now turns his sensitive eye to children, with a special menu and a child-height buffet of kid favorites for the popular Sunday brunch. ◆As befits a restaurant in San Francisco's only hotel to receive both the Mobil Five-Star and AAA Five-Diamond Award for six consecutive years, the wine list is out-standing, a consistent winner of *The Wine Spectator* Grand Award.

AVERAGE DINNER FOR TWO: $95
DOES NOT INCLUDE WINE, TAX AND GRATUITY

HARRIS'

◆

2100 VAN NESS AVENUE
AT PACIFIC AVENUE
SAN FRANCISCO, CA 94109
(415) 673-1888

Major Credit Cards
Open Daily for Dinner • Lunch Wednesday

Proprietor
ANN LEE HARRIS

Chef
GOETZ BOJE

Menu Highlights

Appetizers
HOUSEMADE
COUNTRY-STYLE BEEF
PATÉ • BLUE POINT
OYSTERS • CAVIAR
SERVED ON AN ICE
MOLD • CAESAR SALAD

Entrées
THE HARRIS STEAK •
ROAST PRIME RIB •
GRILLED BREAST OF
CHICKEN • ROAST
DUCKLING À LA
BOJE • FRESH CATCH
OF THE DAY •
MAINE LOBSTER

POPULAR VOTE RATES HARRIS' ONE OF THE BEST STEAKHOUSES in San Francisco. Midwestern corn-fed beef, dry aged for twenty-one days to develop flavor and tenderness, is the specialty at this handsome, high-ceilinged restaurant with comfortable booth seating. A turn-of-the-century bar sets the scene for award-winning martinis and a light supper menu, while the spacious Skylight Room accommodates private parties of up to 100 guests. ◆ Chef Goetz Boje prepares a wide selection of grilled meats and seafood, and an in-house baker creates the popular decadent chocolate cake and the apple and pecan pies. The restaurant's steaks, sausages and rich pâté are available for purchase at the meat counter. ◆ The wine list includes an extensive selection of California Cabernets and Merlots, ideal companions to the robust, beef-oriented fare.

AVERAGE DINNER FOR TWO: $75
DOES NOT INCLUDE WINE, TAX AND GRATUITY

HOUSE OF PRIME RIB

◆

1906 VAN NESS AVENUE
NEAR JACKSON
SAN FRANCISCO, CA 94109
(415) 885-4605

Major Credit Cards
Open Daily • Dinner Only

Proprietor
JOE BETZ

Chef
SALVADOR RODRIGUEZ

Menu Highlights

Entrées

KING HENRY VIII
CUT OF PRIME BEEF •
HOUSE OF PRIME RIB
CUT • PRIME RIB À LA
CARTE • FRESH FISH:
CATCH OF THE DAY • ALL
PRIME RIB DINNERS
SERVED WITH SALAD,
MASHED OR BAKED
POTATOES, YORKSHIRE
PUDDING, CREAMED
SPINACH & FRESH
HORSERADISH SAUCE

THE HOUSE OF PRIME RIB WAS A SAN FRANCISCO INSTITU-
tion, under the same management for thirty-seven years. Now it
seems headed for another long and prosperous reign under proprietor
Joe Betz. ◆ In a complete remodeling, Betz decorated the interior
with light, airy pastel colors and added brass-etched glass to recreate
the atmosphere of an English pub. The specialty of the kitchen, however, has not changed. Each year at House of Prime Rib, some ninety
tons of Eastern corn-fed beef are cured with a secret herb blend from
England, packed in rock salt and roasted in seasoned ovens. The
result: thick, juicy slices of prime rib, cooked to order and artfully
carved from gleaming service carts at the table. ◆ Chef Salvador
Rodriguez, who has presided in the kitchen here for many years, prepares each prime rib dinner and the accompaniments, as well as a fresh
fish of the day. The pecan pie and other temptations from the dessert
cart are worth the extra calories.

AVERAGE DINNER FOR TWO: $45
DOES NOT INCLUDE WINE, TAX AND GRATUITY

IL FORNAIO

◆

1265 BATTERY STREET
LEVI PLAZA
SAN FRANCISCO, CA 94111
(415) 986-0100

MasterCard & Visa Only
Open Daily • Breakfast, Lunch & Dinner

General Manager
GIORGIO VANZULLI

Executive Chef
BARRY MONATH

Menu Highlights

Appetizers
THINLY SLICED SEARED BEEF, GRANA, GREEN PEPPERCORNS & ROSEMARY • THIN, GRILLED BABY EGGPLANT SLICES WITH SUNDRIED TOMATOES, ONIONS & BALSAMIC VINEGAR

Entrées
BAKED LASAGNA LAYERED WITH DUCK RAGOUT, BÉCHAMEL & HERBS • ITALIAN SAUSAGES, STEWED PEPPERS, GRILLED POLENTA • OAKWOOD-ROASTED CHICKEN WITH PANCETTA, GARLIC & LEMON

VISIBLE THROUGH THE SYCAMORE TREES LINING LEVI PLAZA is a landmark brick building that survived the 1906 earthquake. It is a fitting home for Il Fornaio, one of San Francisco's most genuine Italian restaurants. ◆ Il Fornaio, which means "the baker" in Italian, is a combination cafe, bakery, pizzeria, bar and restaurant that attracts an all-day flow of customers with its housemade sweets, rustic breads, cappuccino, pasta and Tuscan-style meats. Grand, arched windows and a glass-enclosed patio face the plaza's waterfall and a seemingly Mediterranean sky. Inside, low lights and golden cherub paintings create a Florentine amber glow that completes the Italian fantasy. ◆ Formerly at Berkeley's Chez Panisse, Executive Chef Barry Monath gathers recipes that preserve the quality and tradition of Italian regional cuisine. Fish and fowl from the rotisserie, wood-roasted game, crispy pizza and tasty sausage plates are just a sampling of the pleasures in store at Il Fornaio.

AVERAGE DINNER FOR TWO: $45
DOES NOT INCLUDE WINE, TAX AND GRATUITY

IMPERIAL PALACE

◆

919 GRANT AVENUE
AT WASHINGTON
SAN FRANCISCO, CA 94108
(415) 982-4440

Major Credit Cards
Open Daily • Lunch & Dinner

Proprietor
TOMMY TOY

Chef
KANCHIU TSE

Menu Highlights

Appetizers
IMPERIAL SPARERIBS
MARINATED WITH PLUM
SAUCE & BARBECUED IN
WINE & HONEY GLAZE

Entrées
IMPERIAL TREAT:
CRABMEAT PUFF WITH
PLUM SAUCE, SOUP
IMPERIAL, ALMOND
CHICKEN, SWEET & SOUR
PORK • EMPEROR'S
GOURMET: TOSSED
CHICKEN IMPERIAL,
BAKED CLAMS, SHREDDED
SCALLOP SOUP, LOBSTER
IMPERIAL, LICHEE
CHICKEN, FOUR
SEASONS RICE

IN THE CENTER OF SAN FRANCISCO'S CHINATOWN IS TOMMY Toy's Imperial Palace, an elegant Oriental setting that has attracted an impressive celebrity clientele over the years. Rich red and gold tones enhance the dining room, where a collection of Ming Dynasty porcelain is displayed in a recessed case. The entryway is lined with autographed pictures of the stars who have dined here, from Barbra Streisand to Bette Midler. ♦ Toy is an energetic impresario, greeting guests and keeping close watch over the kitchen, where Chef Kanchiu Tse oversees the production of authentic Mandarin, Cantonese and Hunan dishes. Each course is impeccably served from a handcarved wood cart rolled to the table. ♦ Like his other fine restaurant, Tommy Toy's, the Imperial Palace reflects Toy's knowledge and appreciation of wine with a well-balanced selection of California vintages.

AVERAGE DINNER FOR TWO: $45
DOES NOT INCLUDE WINE, TAX AND GRATUITY

ONE WORD CAPTURES THE MOMENT.
MUMM'S THE WORD.

Mumm Cordon Rouge. The only champagne to wear the red ribbon, symbol of France's highest honor.
To send a gift of Mumm Champagne, call 1-800-238-4373. Void where prohibited.

XO
COURVOISIER
COGNAC
Courvoisier
750 ML
40% ALC/VOL (80 PROOF)
PRODUCT OF FRANCE
PRODUCED AND BOTTLED BY COURVOISIER, JARNAC, FRANCE

JANOT'S

◆

44 CAMPTON PLACE
AT UNION SQUARE
SAN FRANCISCO, CA 94108
(415) 392-5373

Major Credit Cards
Closed Sunday • Lunch & Dinner

Proprietor/Host
JACQUES JANOT

Chef/Proprietor
PIERRE MORIN

Menu Highlights

Appetizers
SEAFOOD SAUSAGE WITH
WARM CABBAGE SALAD •
GRILLED QUAIL WITH
SMOKED BACON &
SPINACH SALAD

Entrées
BREAST OF CHICKEN
WITH HORSERADISH
SAUCE & CHIVES •
ROLLED FILET OF SOLE
STUFFED WITH SPINACH
& TARRAGON, WHITE
BUTTER SAUCE •
PRAWNS, SCALLOPS &
OYSTERS MOLDED IN
CABBAGE LEAVES,
FENNEL BUTTER SAUCE

THE EPITOME OF FRANCO-CALIFORNIA STYLE, JANOT'S IS A favorite downtown rendezvous by day and an upbeat dinner house by night. Brick walls, brass rails and dark green banquettes exude warmth and neatness, setting a perfect background for the polished cuisine of Chef/proprietor Pierre Morin. ◆ It may have seemed risky for Morin and his partner Jacques Janot to open a French restaurant when California cuisine was the talk of the town. But these two veterans of the San Francisco restaurant business knew exactly what they were doing. Using French techniques, a very quick cooking style and a fresh approach inspired by California's agricultural plenitude, they created an ideal blend. ◆ Three years later, critics from every major publication, from *Gourmet* and *Esquire* to the *San Francisco Chronicle* and the *New York Times*, were unanimous: Janot's impeccable look and superb light fare were just what San Francisco needed.

AVERAGE DINNER FOR TWO: $50
DOES NOT INCLUDE WINE, TAX AND GRATUITY

KULETO'S

◆

VILLA FLORENCE HOTEL
221 POWELL STREET
SAN FRANCISCO, CA 94102
(415) 397-7720

Major Credit Cards
Open Daily for Breakfast, Lunch & Dinner

Manager
PETE SITTNICK

Executive Chef
ROBERT HELSTROM

Menu Highlights

Appetizers
ROASTED GARLIC &
CAMBAZOLA WITH
ROSEMARY PIZZA
BREAD • GRILLED
RADICCHIO & PANCETTA

Entrées
BREAST OF CHICKEN
STUFFED WITH
RICOTTA & HERBS,
ROASTED PEPPER BUTTER
SAUCE • CAPPELLINI
WITH ROMA
TOMATOES, BASIL &
GARLIC • SAFFRON
RISOTTO WITH
PRAWNS, SCALLOPS &
SUNDRIED TOMATOES

KULETO'S IS AN ACTION-PACKED RESTAURANT WITH UP-TO-date Italian food and one of the most inviting bars in town. Forty feet of mahogany, it survived the 1906 quake in the Palace Hotel only to be put in storage. Designer Pat Kuleto, for whom the restaurant is named, refurbished it, hung garlic, dried herbs, salamis — even whole hams — above it, and set a warm, spirited tone that never gets tiring. ◆ Kuleto's and the Villa Florence Hotel are owned by Bill Kimpton, the man behind other successful restaurant/hotel duos such as Masa's/Hotel Vintage Court and Corona Bar & Grill/Monticello Inn. After pioneering the menu at Corona, Chef Bob Helstrom, 33, was sent to Italy to learn the secrets of Italian cuisine. He cures his own prosciutto, makes mozzarella, vinegar, breads and desserts in house, and buys the best extra-virgin olive oil to set on every table. ◆ "In Italy, I learned that food is best kept simple and natural," he explains. "Here, we are a little more eclectic, but the accent is always on freshness."

AVERAGE DINNER FOR TWO: $50
DOES NOT INCLUDE WINE, TAX AND GRATUITY

LASCAUX

◆

248 SUTTER STREET
AT GRANT
SAN FRANCISCO, CA 94108
(415) 391-1555

Major Credit Cards
Closed Sunday • Lunch & Dinner

Manager
PEGGY O'BRIEN

Chef
STEPHEN SILVA
Chef de Cuisine
SCOTT SHULL

Menu Highlights

Appetizers
SUNDRIED TOMATO &
BASIL TORTA WITH
MASCARPONE & GOAT
CHEESES • GRILLED
PRAWNS WITH FAVA BEAN
SALAD & GARLIC-MINT
VINAIGRETTE

Entrées
SPIT-ROASTED SADDLE OF
LAMB SERVED IN ITS
NATURAL JUICES • RABBIT
BRAISED WITH TOMATOES,
CREME FRAICHE &
ROASTED GARLIC •
GRILLED BREAST OF DUCK
WITH ARUGULA, ORANGE
& WALNUT SALAD

THE SUBTERRANEAN LASCAUX, NAMED AFTER THE CAVE IN France containing some of the oldest drawings known to man, is as intriguing as its namesake. Created by renowned designer Pat Kuleto, its interior captures the feel of a real cave, with textured "stone" walls and arched ceilings, a hand-cut French limestone fireplace and pale alabaster wall sconces. Warm, rich colors and soft lighting contribute a sense of elegance, while bas-relief reproductions of Lascaux's prehistoric cave paintings add a rustic touch. ◆ Lascaux's romantic setting is further enhanced by the sounds of live jazz six nights a week, and by original nineteenth and twentieth century artwork from the city's respected Montgomery Gallery. ◆ Chef Stephen Silva, with Chef de Cuisine Scott Shull, brings the south of France alive with Mediterranean offerings that celebrate the freshness of the season.

AVERAGE DINNER FOR TWO: $50
DOES NOT INCLUDE WINE, TAX AND GRATUITY

LA FOLIE

◆

2316 POLK STREET
AT GREEN
SAN FRANCISCO, CA 94109
(415) 776-5577

Major Credit Cards
Closed Sunday • Dinner Only

☎ ☺

Maître d'
GEORGES PASSOT
Proprietor
JAMIE PASSOT

Chef/Proprietor
ROLAND PASSOT

Menu Highlights

Appetizers
RAVIOLI OF SEA
SCALLOPS & SHIITAKE
MUSHROOMS WRAPPED IN
CABBAGE WITH CITRUS
BUTTER & CHIVES •
CRABCAKES WITH ORANGE
VINAIGRETTE

Entrées
ROTI OF QUAIL, WRAPPED
IN CRISPY POTATO
STRINGS • SLICED BREAST
OF DUCK WITH
CALVADOS SAUCE, SERVED
WITH APPLES AND PINE
NUTS • JOHN DORY WITH
A SCALE OF POTATOES
& PARSLEY

SINCE LA FOLIE OPENED THREE YEARS AGO, SAN FRANCISCO'S best chefs and restaurateurs have been spending their nights off sampling Roland Passot's creations. Roland's talent for strong, flavorful cuisine matched by bold presentations is known from his days at Le Français in Chicago, San Francisco's now-closed Chez Michel, and the top restaurants of Lyon, France. ◆ "I call my cooking spontaneous," says the genial Roland. "I never know what I'm going to prepare until after I call my suppliers." ◆ The dining room, with clouds painted on a blue ceiling and monkeys and parrots cavorting on yellow drapes, is crazy enough to convey the "folly" implied by the restaurant's name, yet as warm and inviting as a family-run restaurant should be. Roland's wife, Jamie, is the friendly hostess. Brother Georges, the maître d' and sommelier, has assembled a unique wine list featuring outstanding, little-known French and California selections at great prices.

AVERAGE DINNER FOR TWO: $75
DOES NOT INCLUDE WINE, TAX AND GRATUITY

LA PERGOLA

2060 CHESTNUT STREET
AT STEINER
SAN FRANCISCO, CA 94123
(415) 563-4500

Major Credit Cards
Open Daily • Dinner Only

Proprietor
SANDRA SIEBERT

Chef/Proprietor
GIANCARLO BORTOLOTTI

Menu Highlights

Appetizers
FRESH GRILLED
VEGETABLES MARINATED
IN OLIVE OIL
& HERBS • STEAMED
CRAB, MUSSELS
& CLAMS SERVED
IN SPICY
TOMATO SAUCE

Entrées
SPINACH & EGG
PASTA WITH FRESH
SEAFOOD IN LIGHT
SAUCE • PASTA FILLED
WITH SQUASH IN
BUTTER & SAGE
SAUCE TOPPED WITH
AMARETTO COOKIE

GIANCARLO BORTOLOTTI LEARNED HIS PROFESSION AT A tender age. "When I was a boy, my mother had no time to cook, so she taught me how," says the chef/owner of La Pergola. Necessity soon turned to passion, and twenty years later, although he is far from his childhood village, his uncompromised regional fare remains close to home. ♦ After posts as chef in several prominent San Francisco restaurants, Bortolotti purchased La Pergola with his wife, Sandra Siebert, in 1988. He composes his dishes carefully, and perfects a recipe for months before putting it on his seasonal menu. Bortolotti likes to "design meals for customers who leave the entire selection of food and wine to me." He selects from a mostly Italian wine cellar that is stocked with unusual vintages within a broad price range. ♦ La Pergola's light-hearted atmosphere captures the Italian spirit of making every meal a special occasion. Sponge-painted cream walls, neat round tables and dimmed track lights achieve an uncluttered effect perfect for casual yet serious dining.

AVERAGE DINNER FOR TWO: $50
DOES NOT INCLUDE WINE, TAX AND GRATUITY

L'AVENUE

3854 GEARY BOULEVARD
AT THIRD AVENUE
SAN FRANCISCO, CA 94118
(415) 386-1555

Major Credit Cards
Open Daily • Dinner Only

Chef/Proprietor
NANCY OAKES

Chefs
**GAINES DOBBINS
PAMELA STUDENT**

Menu Highlights

Appetizers
MARYLAND CRABCAKES •
LOBSTER CAPELLINI
FRITTERS WITH TOMATO-
BASIL VINAIGRETTE &
BLACK PEPPER AIOLI

Entrées
GRILLED MONKFISH, WITH
GOLDEN TOMATO SAUCE,
RISOTTO VERDE & MIXED
BABY BEANS SAUTÉED WITH
GARLIC & ROASTED RED
PEPPER • ROASTED &
GRILLED DOUBLE-CUT PORK
LOIN CHOP, WITH MOREL
SAUCE, MORELS, NEW
POTATOES, PEARL ONIONS,
SUMMER SQUASH, BABY
BEETS, GARLIC & HERBS

"THIS IS NOT A THEME-PARK RESTAURANT," SAYS NANCY Oakes, the forthright chef/owner of L'Avenue. "It's for people who really appreciate food, without all the gimmicks." ◆ Simple yet stylish, the small dining room has wood floors, bentwood chairs, creamy yellow walls and a comfortable bar. It's a fitting milieu for the honest, generous food Oakes creates, what some call "New American Bistro" fare. ◆ Oakes learned to cook in a bar (Pat O'Shea's next door), and in nine years gradually weaned her meat-and-potatoes fans from pot roast and hamburgers to pasta and fish. But she never abandoned the basics, and at L'Avenue, the small daily menu always features at least one heartily portioned meat dish. ◆ With talented help in the kitchen — Pamela Student, formerly at Café Mozart, and Gaines Dobbins, from the Commander's Palace in New Orleans — Oakes can lavish attention on every dish. She fills her plates to the edges with intricate, perfectly executed accompaniments. Her fruit desserts, from cobblers to crisps, are outstanding.

AVERAGE DINNER FOR TWO: $55
DOES NOT INCLUDE WINE, TAX AND GRATUITY

Ferrarelle has always enhanced a good meal.

Italians have enjoyed Ferrarelle® mineral water for a long, long time. After all, *these are some of the lightest little bubbles nature has to offer. Not too flat, not too fizzy, Ferrarelle goes perfectly with any food. Even a peeled grape.*

Introducing a class of vodka you never knew existed.

L'OLIVIER

◆

465 DAVIS STREET
NEAR JACKSON
SAN FRANCISCO, CA 94111
(415) 981-7824

Major Credit Cards
Dinner Mon-Sat • Lunch Mon-Fri

☎ 🍸 🚗 🍴 ⓥ 🅿

Proprietors
CHRISTIAN FRANCOZ
GUY FRANCOZ

Chef
ERIC BRANGER

Menu Highlights

Appetizers
FROG LEGS SOUP • COLD
BAKED TOMATO WITH
SMOKED SALMON COULIS •
FEUILLETÉ OF LOBSTER
WITH SAUTERNES-
PAPRIKA SAUCE

Entrées
BAKED ROULADE OF
PETRALE SOLE WITH
TAGLIARINI, GLAZED WITH
SAUVIGNON BLANC
SAUCE • RABBIT
CASSEROLE WITH LEEK,
TOMATO & DIJON
MUSTARD • ROASTED
SQUAB WITH SHIITAKES &
APPLE VINEGAR SAUCE

L'OLIVIER IS A POPULAR BUSINESS-LUNCH PLACE FOR EXECU-
tives by day and a romantic dining spot by night. As soon as one enters
through the large solarium filled with greenery and fresh flowers, one
senses the relaxing, sensuous and elegant ambiance. The main dining
room, decorated with a French provincial fabric and French antiques,
has a quiet, inviting atmosphere. ◆ Proprietors Christian and Guy
Francoz offer a traditional French menu, with adroit and pleasant service from a young staff. Chef Eric Branger, who came to San
Francisco from Florida, trained for three years with Paul Bocuse in
France. He continues L'Olivier's culinary tradition of recipes that are
classical, yet light and low in calories. The desserts, on the other hand,
are superbly rich. ◆ Featuring the most current California selections
as well as renowned French vintages, L'Olivier's wine list is a pleasure
to peruse.

AVERAGE DINNER FOR TWO: $60
DOES NOT INCLUDE WINE, TAX AND GRATUITY

LE PIANO ZINC

◆

708 14TH STREET
AT MARKET
SAN FRANCISCO, CA 94114
(415) 431-5266

Major Credit Cards
Open Daily • Lunch & Dinner

Proprietor
JOEL COUTRE

Chef/Proprietor
MICHEL LAURENT

Menu Highlights

Appetizers
WARM DUCK PATÉ IN PUFF
PASTRY, HONEY &
VINEGAR SAUCE • COLD
TERRINE OF SALMON,
HERB SAUCE • TARTLET
FILLED WITH ESCARGOTS,
WILD MUSHROOMS
& ROQUEFORT

Entrées
STEAMED SEA BASS WITH
FENNEL, ANISE AROMA •
LAMB STEW WITH SMALL
VEGETABLES • BONELESS
RABBIT GRAND VENEUR •
CHICKEN SUPREME WITH
CHANTERELLES,
CHAMPAGNE SAUCE

SINCE IT OPENED ALMOST FIVE YEARS AGO, LE PIANO ZINC has kept abreast of trends without losing its commitment to fine cuisine. In its latest incarnation, this friendly restaurant acknowledges the fast-paced '90s with a new menu available to go, optional delivery to your door, continuous service from 11 a.m. to 11 p.m., and credit card orders sent by fax. Now a romantic dinner at home or a first-class lunch in the office are only a phone call away. ◆ Prices have been lowered, but nothing else about Chef Michel Laurent's fresh, honest cooking has changed. Whether it's a simple warm goat cheese salad, a long-simmered osso bucco or a state-of-the-art flourless chocolate cake, his dishes are perfect compositions of flavor, texture and color. ◆ From the moment proprietor/host Joel Coutre greets his guests with a Kir Royal, to the last, leisurely sip of espresso, Le Piano Zinc delivers the authentic brasserie ambiance San Franciscans have come to love.

AVERAGE DINNER FOR TWO: $40
DOES NOT INCLUDE WINE, TAX AND GRATUITY

MASA'S

648 BUSH STREET
NEAR STOCKTON
SAN FRANCISCO, CA 94108
(415) 989-7154

Major Credit Cards
Closed Sunday & Monday • Dinner Only

Manager
NICK PEYTON

Chef
JULIAN SERRANO

Menu Highlights

Appetizers
FRESH SAUTÉED
FOIE GRAS WITH
TRUFFLES & SPINACH •
TOURNEDOS OF
BABY MAINE LOBSTER
WITH FRESH PASTA &
RED WINE SAUCE

Entrées
ROASTED SQUAB WITH
FRESH CHESTNUT
PURÉE & FLAN OF
CORN & WILD RICE •
SAUTÉED MIGNONS
OF VEAL WITH
ROASTED RED PEPPER
MOUSSE, FRESH
TRUFFLES & MORELS

THE MEMORY OF MASTER CHEF MASATAKI KOBAYASHI GUIDES Chef Julian Serrano as he carries on the visual and gastronomic artistry at Masa's. Together with Manager Nick Peyton and owner Bill Kimpton, Serrano has maintained the impeccable standards set by Masa. Trained in Madrid, Serrano worked with Masa for three years: "I express myself within the unique style and tradition he set." ◆ The magic at Masa's is a combination of aesthetic flair and outstanding cooking; there is so much on each plate, so carefully presented, that it takes at least sixteen people in the kitchen to create fewer than 100 dinners each night. ◆ The wine list is outstanding, and a modest bar serves an extensive California and French selection. Where else could you find Château d'Yquem by the glass?

AVERAGE DINNER FOR TWO: $136
DOES NOT INCLUDE WINE, TAX AND GRATUITY

MASONS

◆

FAIRMONT HOTEL
950 MASON STREET
SAN FRANCISCO, CA 94108
(415) 392-0113

Major Credit Cards
Closed Sunday • Dinner Only

| *General Manager* | *Chef* |
| JACK JENKINS | CLAUDE BOUGARD |

Menu Highlights

Appetizers
JOHN DORY WITH FRESH
PASTA ON A NEST OF
GREENS, SERVED IN
LEMON & HERB
DRESSING • SALMON &
LOBSTER TERRINE WITH
LOBSTER HERB SAUCE

Entrées
LAMB CHOP WRAPPED IN
VEGETABLE MOUSSE,
SERVED WITH THYME-
SCENTED RED WINE
SAUCE • FRESH LOBSTER
SLICED & FANNED OVER
HOMEMADE PASTA,
SERVED WITH
TARRAGON SAUCE

COMPLETELY RENOVATED, MASONS HAS THE LOOK OF A RES-
idential dining room, with comfortable banquettes, lovely window
tables, etched glass and an expanse of blond Japanese butterfly oak.
◆ Chef Claude Bougard, formerly of L'Etoile, has designed a menu
that features California cuisine in a French style. The freshest ingredients shine through in broiled or sautéed dishes, presented in elegantly simple arrangements. The three-course Sunset Menu and
Late Supper Menu, served until 1 a.m. on Friday and Saturday, add
another dimension to this relaxed, elegant restaurant. ◆ Another
alluring draw is nationally recognized Peter Mintun at the piano,
performing in the bar Wednesday through Saturday nights. On
Monday and Tuesday, "Cabaret Singer of the Year" Weslia Whitfield
performs with husband-pianist Michael Greensill.

AVERAGE DINNER FOR TWO: $80
DOES NOT INCLUDE WINE, TAX AND GRATUITY

NOB HILL RESTAURANT

◆

MARK HOPKINS INTER-CONTINENTAL
ONE NOB HILL
SAN FRANCISCO, CA 94108
(415) 391-9362

Major Credit Cards
Breakfast, Lunch & Dinner Daily • Sunday Brunch

Food & Beverage Manager
JEAN-LUC MAUMUS

Executive Chef
TONY BREEZE

Menu Highlights

Appetizers
SAUTÉED DUCK FOIE
GRAS WITH ARTICHOKE
& SORREL RAGOUT •
SALAD OF DUCK
CARPACCIO, WARM
CHEVRE &
TOMATO CONFIT

Entrées
ROASTED ATLANTIC
MONKFISH WITH
RICARD & LEEKS •
ROASTED LOIN OF
LAMB MARINATED
WITH FRESH HERBS,
SERVED WITH
RATATOUILLE

THE STATELY MARK HOPKINS INTER-CONTINENTAL HOTEL
has many claims to fame: a prestigious address, grand views and the
Nob Hill Restaurant, where celebrities and heads of state have dined
for more than thirty years. Softly lit and elegantly paneled in walnut,
it upholds its standard of excellence with outstanding, original cuisine. ◆ Nob Hill's goal, says Chef Ward Little, is "to prepare food that
doesn't follow the latest trend, but pays respect to the long tradition
of great chefs and their accomplishments." To achieve this, Chef
Little and Executive Chef Tony Breeze use the best California meats,
seafood and produce, and insist on just-picked herbs from the hotel's
own garden for their seasonal menu. "Everything is cooked very
fresh," says Breeze, "with no complicated presentations to slow service." ◆ The Nob Hill places equal importance on its wines. One of
the largest Cruvinet preserving and dispensing systems on the West
Coast allows the restaurant to offer an exceptional variety of premium
wines by the glass, each with full bouquet and flavor.

AVERAGE DINNER FOR TWO: $75
DOES NOT INCLUDE WINE, TAX AND GRATUITY

1001 NOB HILL

◆

1001 CALIFORNIA STREET
AT MASON
SAN FRANCISCO, CA 94108
(415) 441-1001

Major Credit Cards
Open Daily • Dinner Only

Proprietors
LEONCE &
CAROLYN PICOT

Chef
EMILE LABROUSSE

Menu Highlights

Appetizers
WARM TERRINE OF WILD
MUSHROOMS • TUNA
TARTARE WITH TAMARI,
WASABI & VEGETABLE
CHIPS • PAN-FRIED
OYSTERS WITH LEMON
BUTTER & ENDIVE

Entrées
DUCK CONFIT, WILD RICE
& BRAISED CABBAGE •
OVEN-ROASTED SALMON
WITH CASSOULET BEANS •
ROASTED RACK OF LAMB
WITH RATATOUILLE
PROVENÇAL • GRILLED
AHI TUNA • STEAMED
MAINE LOBSTER

EVEN WITH THREE OUTSTANDING RESTAURANTS IN FLORIDA and one in Monterey, Leonce Picot dreamed of owning a restaurant in San Francisco. When the old Alexis closed on Nob Hill, he knew he had found the perfect spot. ◆ For a year before 1001 Nob Hill opened in January, 1990, Picot and wife/partner Carolyn worked with California's finest artisans to create an interior that would reflect the city's cross-cultural heritage. They uncovered huge windows and had them paned in beveled glass. They commissioned wrought-iron railings forged by hand, a fireplace faux-finished to Victorian splendor, and murals of Italian street scenes from the inimitable Carlo Marchiori. To hold the restaurant's 9,000 bottles of premium wine, they ordered custom-made redwood wine racks for two spectacular cellar rooms. ◆ In these opulent yet comfortable surroundings, Chef Emile Labrousse puts forth dishes that balance French, Italian and Oriental influences for a fresh San Francisco style. Neither too modern nor too cautious, his culinary combinations always make sense.

AVERAGE DINNER FOR TWO: $90
DOES NOT INCLUDE WINE, TAX AND GRATUITY

Where the Asian style of service meets the American tradition of hospitality.

The Pan Pacific Hotel San Francisco is known not simply for personal valets and chauffeured Rolls-Royces. But also for the warmth and attentiveness of our staff. We're known for the culinary art of our Pacific Grill. As well as the art that adorns our walls.

So call (415) 771-8600. Ask about a weekend stay, or a romantic dinner. You'll find we have a lot to offer.

THE PAN PACIFIC HOTEL
San Francisco

PACIFIC GRILL

◆

PAN PACIFIC HOTEL
500 POST STREET
SAN FRANCISCO, CA 94102
(415) 771-8600

Major Credit Cards
Open Daily • Breakfast, Lunch & Dinner

Managing Director
ROBERT WILHELM

Executive Chef
HANS WIEGAND

Menu Highlights

Appetizers
SPRING ROLLS:
MARINATED SHRIMP IN
GINGER & GARLIC WITH
NAPA CABBAGE, ROLLED
IN ORIENTAL PASTA,
SERVED WITH BLACK BEAN
SAUCE • ROLLED SMOKED
SALMON IN NORI, WITH
SOUR CREAM & CAVIAR

Entrées
NEW YORK BLACK ANGUS
STRIP WITH FRESH
CRACKED PEPPERCORNS &
PACIFIC RATATOUILLE •
BREAST OF CHICKEN WITH
RED PEPPERS & A TANGY
CILANTRO SAUCE

SET IN THE TAN MARBLE LOBBY OF THE PAN PACIFIC HOTEL, formerly the Portman, the Pacific Grill conveys a friendly, informal atmosphere. It's a relaxing place to go before or after the theatre, and its roomy tables make it a refuge of calm at lunch or breakfast. ◆ Known for its first-class hotels in the Orient, the Pan Pacific enters the San Francisco market with confidence. Part of that comes from having the right people: Managing Director Robert Wilhelm has brought not only his many years of experience at the Westin St. Francis Hotel, but also his favorite chef, Hans Wiegand. A native of Frankfurt, Germany, Chef Wiegand was executive sous chef at the St. Francis, then helped put the Westin Hotel in Ottawa on the map. ◆ Here, he introduces a sophisticated touch of Pacific Rim ingredients to a menu that emphasizes lightness. "I don't like aggressive flavors," he explains. "You should be able to taste the freshness of everything." One bite of his crabcakes, made with flaky blue crab instead of Dungeness, quickly proves him right.

AVERAGE DINNER FOR TWO: $80
DOES NOT INCLUDE WINE, TAX AND GRATUITY

ORITALIA

◆

1915 FILLMORE STREET
AT PINE
SAN FRANCISCO, CA 94115
(415) 346-1333

MasterCard & Visa Only
Open Daily • Dinner Only

Proprietor
NORI YOSHIDA

Chef
JOHN ESTRADA

Menu Highlights

Entrées
FRIED SHRIMP & PORK
DUMPLINGS WITH
CILANTRO-MINT SAUCE •
INDONESIAN CHICKEN
SATÉ • KOREAN
BARBECUED BEEF WITH
LETTUCE WRAP • SPICY
MABO-TOFU PASTA
WITH SHIITAKE
MUSHROOMS &
SUNDRIED TOMATOES •
CRABCAKES WITH
ROASTED RED
PEPPER CREAM SAUCE •
ENOKI-SHIITAKE-OYSTER
MUSHROOMS IN SAKE-
BUTTER-GINGER SAUCE

SIX MONTHS BEFORE HE OPENED ORITALIA'S DOORS TO THE public, Nori Yoshida and his chefs were in the kitchen refining his unique blend of Oriental and Italian cuisines. He teamed linguini with *unagi*, shiitake mushrooms with sundried tomatoes, and Chinese noodles with balsamic vinegar and olive oil. The results were satisfying and exotic. Now forming the core of Oritalia's menu, the dishes are served in small portions, dim sum and tapas style, for the ultimate "grazing" experience. ◆ A man of insatiable culinary curiosity, Yoshida travels extensively in search of intriguing flavors. "I consider myself a professional food sampler rather than a restaurateur," says the former owner of Yoshida-Ya. "Since I couldn't find anything like this, I created it myself." ◆ Yoshida masterminded the restaurant's design, a cozy yet classic interior warmed by a huge copper hood over an open kitchen. With flawless service and an eclectic crowd, Oritalia's blend of East and West is San Francisco at its best.

AVERAGE DINNER FOR TWO: $50
DOES NOT INCLUDE WINE, TAX AND GRATUITY

PALIO D'ASTI

640 SACRAMENTO STREET
AT MONTGOMERY
SAN FRANCISCO, CA 94111
(415) 395-9800

Major Credit Cards
Open Daily • Lunch & Dinner

General Manager
TOMMASO BUNKER

Chefs
MARCO FIORINI
MARCELLO BIGOTTI

Menu Highlights

Appetizers
ANTIPASTI FROM THE
CARRELLO • BEEF
CARPACCIO

Entrées
RAVIOLI FILLED WITH
FONTINA CHEESE,
TOASTED ALMONDS
& ESSENCE OF
WHITE TRUFFLES •
GRILLED PRAWNS
WITH WHITE POLENTA •
COHO SALMON BAKED IN
PARCHMENT • BRAISED
SONOMA RABBIT IN
LEMON-EGG SAUCE

AFTER BREATHING NEW LIFE INTO THE BLUE FOX, OWNER Gianni Fassio needed another challenge. He created Palio d'Asti, a restaurant that embodies his vision of Italy: grounded in tradition, yet on the cutting edge of style. ◆ The theme, a bareback horse race (*il palio*) held in Fassio's ancestral home of Asti since 1275, echoes playfully throughout the interior: in the bar curved like a racetrack, in the rough stone columns and staggered ceilings that evoke the streets of Asti, and in the muted medieval colors at play on the surfaces and festive banners. ◆ From San Francisco's sleekest open kitchen comes cuisine as riveting as the design. Italian chefs Marcello Bigotti and Marco Fiorini, with a little help from Fassio's mother, have designed a menu of traditional dishes from Northern Italy. For starters, ask to see the *carrello*, a custom-made antipasti cart. With the turn of a crank, eighteen trays roll by, revealing such delights as caramelized pearl onions, baked mussels and eggplant grilled with olive oil and garlic. ◆ Antipasti and pizzas from a wood-burning oven are served after 11 p.m.

AVERAGE DINNER FOR TWO: $50
DOES NOT INCLUDE WINE, TAX AND GRATUITY

PARK GRILL
◆

PARK HYATT SAN FRANCISCO
333 BATTERY STREET
SAN FRANCISCO, CA 94111
(415) 296-2933

Major Credit Cards
Breakfast, Lunch & Dinner Daily • Sat & Sun Brunch

General Manager
CHERYL PHELPS

Chef
RICK SCOTT

Menu Highlights

Appetizers
AHI TUNA TARTARE WITH TOAST POINTS • WARM DUCK CONFIT WITH FRISÉE, ENDIVE & BUTTER LETTUCE, PAPAYA & LEMON GRASS VINAIGRETTE

Entrées
SAUTÉED PRAWNS WITH THAI SPICES • GRILLED BREAST OF FREE-RANGE CHICKEN ON GRILLED LEEKS • GRILLED LAMB CHOPS, RED CURRANT JUS • LINGUINI WITH SHRIMP, SCALLOPS & MUSSELS

GUESTS WHO APPRECIATE COMFORT, WARMTH AND QUIET sophistication have discovered San Francisco's new Park Hyatt. The Park Grill exudes the same qualities. Australian lacewood, intricate teak and ebony marquetry, and subtly whimsical still lifes create a relaxing backdrop for Chef Rick Scott's deft blend of French, Pacific and regional American cuisines. ◆ Its proximity to the Financial District and the Embarcadero Center makes the Park Grill a natural choice for power lunches (and breakfasts), post-work cocktails or leisurely dining. Since the outcome of a business meeting can often hinge on the success of the meal itself, the Grill provides personal, professional service — and memo pads at each table. Designed with acoustics in mind, the dining room is never noisy, even when filled to capacity. ◆ For those who are on a less demanding schedule, the Grill also serves a daily menu of light fare from 11 a.m. to 1 a.m. in the bar, a traditional afternoon tea, and early evening caviar and oyster service in the lounge.

AVERAGE DINNER FOR TWO: $70
DOES NOT INCLUDE WINE, TAX AND GRATUITY

PIERRE

◆

LE MERIDIEN HOTEL
50 THIRD STREET
SAN FRANCISCO, CA 94103
(415) 974-6400

Major Credit Cards
Closed Sun & Mon • Dinner Only

Food & Beverage Director
JACQUES MURY

Chef
BRUNO LOPEZ

Menu Highlights

Appetizers
LOBSTER CONSOMMÉ
WITH SEA SCALLOPS
MOUSSELINE & VEGETABLE
PEARLS • TRIO OF FOIE
GRAS WITH TOASTED
FRENCH BRIOCHE

Entrées
LAYER OF SEA BASS
FILET WITH POTATO
CAKE & MEDITERRANEAN
HERBS • STEAMED FILET
OF JOHN DORY WITH
VEGETABLE SCALES
& SAFFRON MUSSEL
SAUCE • ROASTED SQUAB
WITH GARLIC FLAN &
BABY VEGETABLES

WHEN THE PIERRE OPENED IN LE MERIDIEN HOTEL IN 1983, it immediately attracted a following among both city residents and visitors. Conveniently located near Union Square, Le Meridien is one of San Francisco's foremost luxury hotels. ◆The Pierre has a genuinely French formality without pretentiousness, presenting gracious and professional service, hand-painted porcelain dinnerware, sparkling crystal glassware and fresh flowers to complement the sumptuous menu. ◆Chef Bruno Lopez achieves a unique balance between classic French and inventive California cuisine. A prix-fixe tasting menu is presented nightly, and several times a year one of France's culinary superstars prepares a series of special dinners as part of Pierre's popular Master Chefs of France program. The expertly researched wine list offers a fine selection of both California and French wines. Enjoy the piano music of Merl Saunders nightly.

AVERAGE DINNER FOR TWO: $85
DOES NOT INCLUDE WINE, TAX AND GRATUITY

POSTRIO

◆

545 POST STREET
NEAR MASON
SAN FRANCISCO, CA 94102
(415) 776-7825

Major Credit Cards
Open Daily • Breakfast, Lunch & Dinner

Chef/Proprietor
ANNE GINGRASS

Chef/Proprietor
DAVID GINGRASS

Menu Highlights

Appetizers
SAUTÉED SCALLOPS
WITH SONOMA GREENS,
POTATO CHIPS & SOY
VINAIGRETTE •
SMOKED DUCK
CARPACCIO WITH
WILTED GREENS &
SHALLOT-BLACK
PEPPER VINAIGRETTE

Entrées
CHINESE-STYLE DUCK
WITH SPICY MANGO
SAUCE ON ARUGULA &
ONIONS • CRISPLY
SAUTÉED SWEETBREADS
WITH ARUGULA &
SHERRY WINE SAUCE

AFTER MONTHS OF SPECULATION AND PRESS ATTENTION, Postrio opened its doors on April 1, 1989, to instant acclaim. The legendary Wolfgang Puck, creator of L.A.'s Spago and Chinois on Main, and Chef/owners Anne and David Gingrass couldn't be happier. "It was very exciting to plan everything for so long," says David, "and have it all work." ◆ Graduates of the Culinary Institute of America, both Gingrasses apprenticed with Puck at Spago. Their distinct style of California cuisine has Asian and Southern European influences and is a bit heartier than the L.A. Spago style. The dramatic Postrio, a Pat Kuleto design, has quickly won a diverse, loyal following of locals and tourists. "We don't discriminate between tuxedoes and blue jeans," David says. ◆ Patrons descend the striking staircase of sculpted iron and copper to the main dining room — where reservations are imperative — or stay upstairs in the bar for a light repast of gourmet pizzas and appetizers, served until 1:30 a.m. Breakfast is another way to sample Postrio's outstanding cuisine.

AVERAGE DINNER FOR TWO: $75
DOES NOT INCLUDE WINE, TAX AND GRATUITY

Your Scotch and Soda
is only as good as your Scotch and soda.

What are you saving the Chivas for?

Elegance with Style

R·E·G·I·S

H O T E L

Just two blocks from Union Square, the Regis Hotel is a gem of rare and uncompromising quality – a quietly elegant boutique hotel in the warmest European tradition. Guest rooms (some with fireplaces) and suites are richly furnished with canopied beds and Louis XVI period pieces. Bathrooms are finished in black Italian marble accented with gleaming brass fixtures. All rooms feature honor-bar refrigerators and hair dryers. Handsome boardroom and conference facilities provide the perfect venue for small to mid-size meetings. The elegant bar and lounge, along with a superb restaurant, ensure a memorable dining experience.

490 Geary Street, San Francisco, California 94102 • (415) 928-7900

REGINA'S

◆

REGIS HOTEL
490 GEARY STREET
SAN FRANCISCO, CA 94102
(415) 885-1661

Major Credit Cards
Dinner Tues-Sun • Lunch Mon-Fri • Sat & Sun Brunch

Proprietor — *Chef/Proprietor*
JAMES LUNSFORD — REGINA CHARBONEAU

Menu Highlights

Appetizers
PEPPERED SHRIMP •
FROMAGE EN CROUTE •
CREOLE CORN CRAB
BISQUE • OYSTERS 2, 2 &
2 (BIENVILLE, OHAN &
ROCKEFELLER)

Entrées
EGGPLANT LAFAYETTE
WITH GULF SHRIMP &
CRAB • CRAWFISH PIE •
LAMB CHOPS WITH
TOMATO-MINT
MARMALADE •
BOUILLABAISSE • DUCK
WITH SEASONED RICE
DRESSING & FIG
PRESERVES

OF A HANDFUL OF RESTAURANTS SERVING "LOUISIANA haute cuisine," Regina's has truly made a name for itself. Located on Theatre Row, the restaurant and convivial lounge are decorated with specially commissioned gold-framed sketches of performers who have graced the local theatre scene since the early 1900s. Commedia masks and colorful costume designs expand the thespian theme. ◆The leading lady in this dramatic setting is Regina Charboneau. Born in Natchez, Mississippi, just up the river from New Orleans, the La Varenne-trained chef has remained true to her French Creole roots, offering spicy yet sophisticated interpretations of New Orleans specialties. ◆Patrons flock to Regina's for the late-night "After the Arts" menu (served until 1 a.m. on weekends). Offering everything from Southern cocktails to rich desserts, it is a perfect encore to an evening at the theatre.

AVERAGE DINNER FOR TWO: $65
DOES NOT INCLUDE WINE, TAX AND GRATUITY

RISTORANTE DONATELLO

◆

501 POST STREET
AT MASON
SAN FRANCISCO, CA 94102
(415) 441-7182

Major Credit Cards
Open Daily • Breakfast & Dinner

Proprietor
A. CAL ROSSI, JR.

Chef
RON MILLER

Menu Highlights

Appetizers
SMOKED STURGEON &
BABY FIELD LETTUCE WITH
OLIVE OIL & LEMON •
ARTICHOKES & PRAWNS
FRICASSÉE WITH BASIL •
GRATINÉED CREAM OF
BORLOTTI BEANS &
BARLEY

Entrées
MAINE LOBSTER
FRICASSEE WITH FENNEL
& CARROT • MEDALLIONS
OF VENISON WITH WILD
MUSHROOMS • VEAL CHOP
IN MADEIRA SAUCE WITH
FRESH ROSEMARY

RISTORANTE DONATELLO IS THE LEADER OF A GROWING CLUSTER of Italian restaurants in Northern California taking a serious look at fine Italian cuisine. Located near Union Square in the elegant Donatello Hotel, the restaurant was named for a leading Italian Renaissance sculptor. Donatello's two dining rooms are distinctively decorated with Venetian glass, marble, Carpaccio lamps, Fortuny fabric panels and an abundance of mirrors. ◆ Creator and owner A. Cal Rossi, Jr., took an early and active role in shaping Donatello's style and standards. His personal involvement carries over into the flawless preparation and presentation of Chef Ron Miller's cuisine. ◆ Donatello also invites some of Italy's finest chefs to preside in its kitchen for one week a year during the annual Visiting Chef Series, giving the staff a rare opportunity to keep abreast of the latest in Italian cooking and allowing guests to experience the featured five-course gastronomic menu and regional wines.

AVERAGE DINNER FOR TWO: $80
DOES NOT INCLUDE WINE, TAX AND GRATUITY

SILKS

MANDARIN ORIENTAL HOTEL
222 SANSOME STREET
SAN FRANCISCO, CA 94104
(415) 986-2020

Major Credit Cards
Breakfast, Lunch & Dinner Daily • Sunday Brunch

Manager	Chef
MICHAEL THORBURN	DAVID KINCH

Menu Highlights

Appetizers
SPICY CUCUMBER SALAD
WITH CRISPY LOBSTER &
SCALLOP WONTONS •
CORIANDER-CURED
SALMON WITH
HORSERADISH CREAM •
GAZPACHO WITH
CUCUMBER ICE &
STEAMED POTATOES

Entrées
SEARED JAPANESE TUNA
WITH LOBSTER & BASIL •
ROASTED RACK OF LAMB
WITH WARM MINT VINAI-
GRETTE • STEAMED
SALMON WITH FRESH
TOMATO & BASIL OIL

VISITORS CROSS AN OPULENT GREEN-AND-WHITE MARBLE lobby and ascend an elegant staircase to reach Silks. The centerpiece of the dining room is an octagonal copper-and-brass table loaded with fruits, vegetables, breads, wines and liqueurs. Attentive waiters pass silently by luxe tables in secluded niches. ◆ In this grand setting, the cuisine comes as a refreshing surprise. The management at the Mandarin Oriental wanted a restaurant that served California cuisine of a caliber that would attract the hard-to-please local clientele. In Silks, they have succeeded. ◆ Chef David Kinch combines the techniques he learned as a working chef at New York's Quilted Giraffe with his Japanese training in the presentation and use of Asian ingredients. "I have a definite Pacific Rim aesthetic — a strong preference for seafood, an abundance of herbs and fresh seasonal produce."

AVERAGE DINNER FOR TWO: $80
DOES NOT INCLUDE WINE, TAX AND GRATUITY

690

◆

690 VAN NESS AVENUE
AT TURK
SAN FRANCISCO, CA 94102
(415) 255-6900

Visa & MasterCard Only
Dinner Daily • Lunch Mon-Fri • Sunday Brunch

General Manager
GLENN PERKINS

Chef
DAVID ROBINS

Menu Highlights

Appetizers
690 SHRIMP ROLL
WITH CUCUMBER,
MINT & SESAME-
ROASTED BELL
PEPPER VINAIGRETTE •
THAI STICKS WITH
MINT & TAMARIND

Entrées
GRILLED SMOKY-CHILE
PACIFIC SNAPPER WITH
MEXICAN BLACK BEANS
& TOMATO SALSA •
SAUTÉED SALMON
WITH ONION RINGS &
MANGO SAUCE

OPENED IN MAY OF 1989, 690 WAS BORN MONTHS BEFORE ON a warm beach in Australia where Jeremiah Tower of Stars had joined Chef David Robins on vacation. After taking over the old Speedo 690 carburetor shop on Van Ness, they created a sun-drenched menu influenced by the spicy tropical food of Southeast Asia and the Caribbean. Always crowded, 690 attracts a lively mix of young people, Civic Center employees and patrons of the arts. "It's not loud and boisterous," says Robins, "but it does have a party feel." ◆ A bright oasis in San Francisco's foggy climate, 690 is scantily clad with a colorfully painted canvas banner of men and women enjoying water sports, and huge windows along two sides. Two bright red English phone booths flank the bar, and beach umbrellas hang above the tables next to the open kitchen, where Robins can be seen in his element. ◆ The menu changes with the whims of its young chef. "If I need ideas," says Robins, "I imagine myself sitting on a beach again."

AVERAGE DINNER FOR TWO: $60
DOES NOT INCLUDE WINE, TAX AND GRATUITY

SQUARE ONE

◆

190 PACIFIC AVENUE
NEAR FRONT
SAN FRANCISCO, CA 94111
(415) 788-1110

Major Credit Cards
Open Daily for Dinner • Lunch Mon-Fri

Proprietor
EVAN GOLDSTEIN

Chef/Proprietor
JOYCE GOLDSTEIN

Menu Highlights

Appetizers
PORTUGUESE CRABCAKES •
BAKED GOAT CHEESE IN
FILO WITH ARUGULA,
GREEN BEANS &
SUNDRIED TOMATO
VINAIGRETTE

Entrées
PAELLA: SAFFRON RICE
WITH LOBSTER, MANILA
CLAMS, CHORIZO,
CHICKEN & ARTICHOKES •
GRILLED SWORDFISH,
MOROCCAN CHARMOULA,
COUSCOUS & GRILLED
VEGETABLES • PROVENÇAL
DUCK WITH LAVENDER
HONEY & THYME

CHEF/OWNER JOYCE GOLDSTEIN'S AWARD-WINNING RESTAURANT has a wonderful view onto the lush greenery of Walton Park and an ambiance as upbeat as its diverse clientele. ◆ "I treat my restaurant like my home," Goldstein says. "I don't like to cook or eat the same things every night. Our guests have come to expect diversity as well as quality." Breads, pastries, ice creams and even condiments are made from scratch, and heart-healthy items are always available. ◆ Square One's daily-changing menu presents a repertoire of classic dishes from around the world, with an emphasis on the robust and sensual cuisine of the Mediterranean. Those in the know book early for Joyce's famous regional Italian dinners, the Wednesday specialty. A nightly appetizer menu is offered in the lively bar, and the private room accommodates up to thirty-five guests. ◆ Imaginative and varied, Square One's award-winning wine list is chosen by Joyce's oenophile son, Evan, 29, the youngest American to gain membership in the prestigious British Court of Master Sommeliers.

AVERAGE DINNER FOR TWO: $65
DOES NOT INCLUDE WINE, TAX AND GRATUITY

STARS

◆

150 REDWOOD ALLEY
NEAR VAN NESS
SAN FRANCISCO, CA 94102
(415) 861-7827

Major Credit Cards
Open Daily • Lunch & Dinner

General Manager
TONY ANGOTTI

Executive Chef
MARK FRANZ
Pastry Chef
EMILY LUCHETTI

Menu Highlights

Appetizers
CORN RAVIOLI WITH
GRILLED LOBSTER,
CHERVIL & FAVA BEANS •
RED & YELLOW TOMATOES
WITH FRIED OKRA, GOAT
CHEESE, PANCETTA &
BASIL PESTO RELISH

Entrées
ROASTED SALMON WITH
SUMMER VEGETABLE
BRUNOISE, LOBSTER
SAUCE, FRIED LEEKS &
TARRAGON AIOLI •
RED WINE-BRAISED
VEAL SHANK WITH
WILD MUSHROOMS
& MOROCCAN
LEMON RELISH

WITHIN A SPACIOUS ROOM HOUSING AN OPEN KITCHEN, TWO elevated dining areas, a grand piano and an always packed cocktail area, Stars shines with an unsurpassed intensity — at the counter, at the tables, on the wine list and, most importantly, in the kitchen. ◆ Behind the restaurant's unique appeal is Chef/owner Jeremiah Tower, who fell in love with cooking at a very early age and later decided food, wine and meeting people were the aspects of life he most enjoyed. In 1972, he became chef at Chez Panisse and later co-owner. ◆ Tower created Stars, near San Francisco's civic and cultural center, to provide performers with a haven of exciting food, wine and ambiance. "San Franciscans like to go to the same place frequently," he says, "but they also need the new and exciting." With the addition of the casual Stars Café and The Grillroom for private parties, Stars has remained exciting — and packed — since it opened in 1984.

AVERAGE DINNER FOR TWO: $70
DOES NOT INCLUDE WINE, TAX AND GRATUITY

DEWAR'S PROFILE:

JEREMIAH TOWER

HOME: San Francisco, California.

AGE: 45.

PROFESSION: Head chef and owner, Stars.

HOBBY: Running the Society to Stamp Out Kiwis. "The fruit, not the bird."

LAST BOOK READ: *Bread and Circuses*, Patrick Brantlinger.

LATEST ACCOMPLISHMENT: Wrote a cookbook, *New American Classics*, featuring such recipes as Eggs in Hell, Texas Style.

WHY I DO WHAT I DO: "With a B.A. and M.A. in architecture from Harvard, it's hard to explain, but it's a lot of fun."

QUOTE: "Fresh herbs."

PROFILE: Aristocratic, confident and a self-described monarchist. "Everyone likes to have things his own way. I just admit it."

HIS SCOTCH: Dewar's® "White Label®" with soda. "I particularly enjoy something I don't have to cook."

TOMMY TOY'S

◆

655 MONTGOMERY STREET
AT WASHINGTON
SAN FRANCISCO, CA 94108
(415) 397-4888

Major Credit Cards
Open Daily for Dinner • Lunch Mon-Fri

Proprietor
TOMMY TOY

Chef
KEN WU

Menu Highlights

Appetizers
PAN-FRIED FOIE
GRAS WITH SLICED
PEAR & WATERCRESS IN
SWEET PICKLED GINGER
SAUCE • LOBSTER
POTSTICKERS WITH
CHILE SAUCE

Entrées
WOK-CHARRED VEAL
IN SZECHUAN SAUCE •
VANILLA PRAWNS
& RAISINS WITH FRESH
MELON • DUCKLING
BREAST SMOKED
WITH CAMPHORWOOD
& TEA LEAVES, PLUM
WINE SAUCE

FIFTEEN YEARS AFTER HE OPENED THE HIGHLY SUCcessful Imperial Palace, Tommy Toy did it again with Tommy Toy's. This time, he created a sumptuous restaurant off the beaten track, "for discriminating people who want an elegant French touch to their Chinese cuisine." ◆ You won't find chopsticks here, only silverware, porcelain, authentic Chinese bridal lamps, and an incomparable display of Chinese pottery and art from the private collection of Toy's partner, Joe Yuey. Toy, trained as an interior decorator, has recreated the opulence of the nineteenth-century Empress Dowager's reading room, with ancient "Powder Paintings" framed in sandalwood and hand-carved antique wood archways from mainland China. ◆ The food here is no less opulent, consisting of Cantonese and Szechuan dishes refined by Toy's own palate. Ask him to design your dinner menu himself, and you will enjoy a most memorable meal.

AVERAGE DINNER FOR TWO: $50
DOES NOT INCLUDE WINE, TAX AND GRATUITY

VICTOR'S

ST. FRANCIS HOTEL
335 POWELL STREET
SAN FRANCISCO, CA 94102
(415) 774-0253

Major Credit Cards
Open Daily for Dinner • Sunday Brunch

Manager/Maitre d'
ANDRE GUERIN

Chef
JOEL RAMBAUD

Menu Highlights

Appetizers

CHEF JOEL'S SONOMA
DUCK FOIE GRAS •
BRAISED FILET OF BABY
SALMON, DRY VERMOUTH
& CHIVE SAUCE • PRAWNS
SCAMPI WITH ESSENCE
OF SAFFRON

Entrées

HOT MESQUITE-SMOKED
RACK OF LAMB ON BEAN
RAGOUT & SWEET GARLIC
SAUCE • MAINE LOBSTER
RAGOUT ON NORTH
BEACH PASTA WITH
MADEIRA SAUCE

ON THE TOP FLOOR OF THE PRESTIGIOUS ST. FRANCIS HOTEL, the award-winning Victor's is a truly special find: a great hotel serving excellent food in a room with a spectacular view. After a breathtaking ride up thirty stories in an outside glass elevator, guests enter an elegant, wood-paneled corridor with recessed bookshelves housing leather-bound classics. In the dining room, floor-to-ceiling windows maximize the view of San Francisco and the bay. ♦ Chef Joel Rambaud, responding to the demands of his guests for California cuisine, has redefined a series of traditional recipes incorporating light sauces made to order with fresh produce from around the world. Dinner, before or after the theatre, is enhanced by selections from a wine cellar that features more than 25,000 bottles. ♦ Sunday brunch at Victor's is a San Francisco tradition that draws a faithful local clientele.

AVERAGE DINNER FOR TWO: $80
DOES NOT INCLUDE WINE, TAX AND GRATUITY

YOSHIDA-YA

◆

2909 WEBSTER STREET
AT UNION
SAN FRANCISCO, CA 94123
(415) 346-3431

Major Credit Cards
Open Daily • Dinner Only

General Manager
KENNY MAKINO

Chef
MASA ENDO

Menu Highlights

Appetizers
CRUNCHY SPICY
CHICKEN WINGS •
RARE BROILED TUNA
WITH GREEN ONION
& LEMON SERVED
WITH SPECIAL CHEF
DRESSING • SUSHI

Entrées
FILET MIGNON
HIBACHI • YAKITORI
DINNER HIBACHI •
SHINKO YAKI
CHICKEN DINNER;
BARBECUED HALF
CHICKEN •
SHABU SHABU

THE INVITING INTERIOR OF YOSHIDA-YA HINTS AT THE TRADI-
tional ambiance found within. Touches of Kyoto red and shades of
apricot appear throughout the serene wood and tile interior. The
ground floor dining room and sushi bar serves sixty kinds of appetizers — sushi, yakitori-grilled chicken, meat and vegetables, and lots of
other tantalizing Japanese tidbits. It's an informal, modern way to
dine. Upstairs, relax at regular tables, or sit on the floor at low tables
over wells, which allow for Western-style comfort. ◆Chef Masa Endo,
a master of traditional Japanese cooking, prepares the famous
Omakase "leave it to the chef" dinner with two days' advance notice.
It is Japanese cuisine, both traditional and original, some of it influenced by the cuisine of other countries. ◆Several times a year, Yoshida-
Ya invites the best chefs of Japan to prepare gala dinners on Japanese
themes. Don't miss them!

AVERAGE DINNER FOR TWO: $50
DOES NOT INCLUDE WINE, TAX AND GRATUITY

ZOLA'S

◆

395 HAYES STREET
AT GOUGH
SAN FRANCISCO, CA 94102
(415) 864-4824

Major Credit Cards
Closed Sunday • Dinner Only

Proprietor
LARRY BAIN

Chef/Proprietor
CATHERINE PANTSIOS
Chef
RACHEL GARDNER

Menu Highlights

Appetizers
SOFT POLENTA WITH
MASCARPONE & GRILLED
WILD MUSHROOMS • MINT
& DILL-CURED SALMON
WITH MELON, CUCUMBERS
& RADISHES • RABBIT
BOUDIN BLANC WITH
APPLE MUSTARD

Entrées
ROASTED BREAST &
CONFIT LEG OF DUCK
WITH FRESH TOMATO-
CALAMATA OLIVE SAUCE •
MORROCCAN SPICED RACK
OF LAMB • PRAWNS,
SCALLOPS & SEA BASS IN
SPICY TOMATO BROTH

WHEN LARRY BAIN AND CATHERINE PANTSIOS MOVED ZOLA'S to fresh new quarters near the Civic Center, they revitalized what was already one of San Francisco's best restaurants. Now a harmonious and spacious interplay of plush carpeting, ochre walls and the latest Italian lighting, Zola's has lost none of its warmth yet has gained an elegance worthy of its cuisine. ◆ Beginning eight years ago as the epitome of French country style, the cooking of Pantsios and Rachel Gardner has evolved into an inspired blend of past and present. The cassoulets and confits are still lovingly prepared according to the demands of time and tradition, but California innovations have added an emphasis on freshness and simplicity. The result is exciting food, as satisfying as it is up to date. ◆ Bain's wine list is a connoisseur's selection of affordable French and California wines. Best of all, the moderate prices and unpretentious ambiance that have made Zola's so popular remain firmly in place.

AVERAGE DINNER FOR TWO: $65
DOES NOT INCLUDE WINE, TAX AND GRATUITY

The art of Pancaldi

The art of Gianfranco Ferre

The art of Fratelli Rossetti

PART OF THE ART

The art of Bottega Veneta

Imported
Product of Italy

Frangelico
liqueur

According to the legend Frangelico lived
three centuries ago in the hilly area found
by the right bank of the river Po.

He lived as a hermit and through his use
of nature and knowledge of its secrets
created unique recipes for liqueurs

The most precious one of all was a liqueur
made from wild hazel nuts with infusions of
berries and flowers to enrich the flavor.

We continue the tradition by
this fine liqueur in honor of

The art of Alessi

Frangelico®
liqueur

The delicate hazelnut liqueur from Italy.

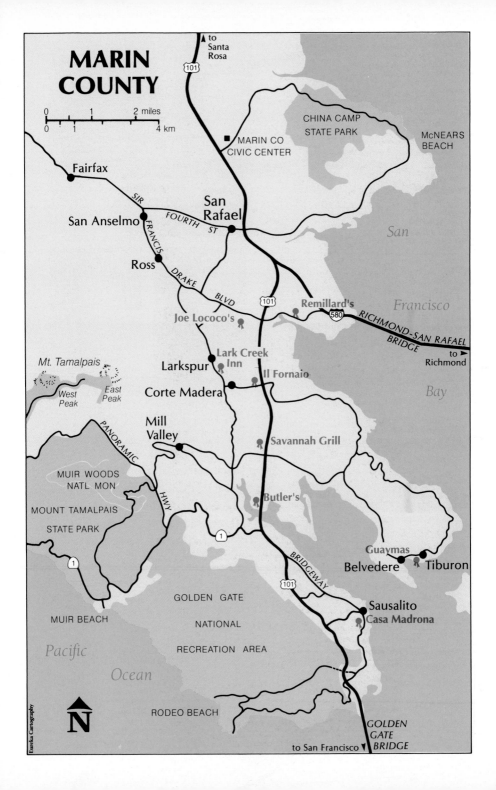

BUTLER'S

◆

625 REDWOOD HIGHWAY
OFF SEMINARY EXIT
MILL VALLEY, CA 94941
(415) 383-1900

Major Credit Cards
Dinner Tues-Sun • Lunch Mon-Fri • Sunday Brunch

Proprietor
ROB BUCKLEY

Chef
ERIK SCHROTH

Menu Highlights

Appetizers
CAESAR SALAD WITH
REGGIANO PARMESAN &
GARLIC CROUTONS •
FRIED CALAMARI SERVED
ON ROASTED TOMATO
SAUCE WITH CILANTRO
PESTO • TUNA NIÇOISE

Entrées
GRILLED PACIFIC COAST
SALMON ON A MEDLEY OF
VEGETABLES SAUTÉED IN
CHERVIL-LIME BUTTER •
SAUTÉED ROCKY RANGE
CHICKEN BREAST COATED
IN CORNMEAL, STUFFED
WITH JALAPEÑO
GOAT CHEESE

OVERLOOKING RICHARDSON BAY, BUTLER'S WINDOWS FRAME a serene landscape of lagoon and tangled hillsides winding to the heights of Mt. Tamalpais and the dramatic sunsets of brilliant color above. As striking is the restaurant's interior, a simple white expanse and long exhibition kitchen, perfumed with the scent of burning mesquite. ◆ Proprietor and host Rob Buckley's dedication assures that Butler's will continue to offer more than just a scenic panorama. Known for its sprightly California style, the changing menu offers expertly grilled or sautéed meats and seafood, enhanced by seasonal vegetable relishes or chutneys instead of sauces. Enticing pastries, puddings, sorbets and ice creams are all made in house. ◆ With the addition of a hearty Sunday brunch, Butler's is now as appealing by day as it is by night.

AVERAGE DINNER FOR TWO: $50
DOES NOT INCLUDE WINE, TAX AND GRATUITY

CASA MADRONA

◆

801 BRIDGEWAY
SAUSALITO, CA 94965
(415) 331-5888

MasterCard & Visa Only
Open Daily for Dinner • Lunch Mon-Fri
Sunday Brunch

Proprietor
JOHN W. MAYS

Chef
KIRKE BYERS

Menu Highlights

Appetizers
HOUSE-CURED GRAVLAX
WITH MARINATED RED
ONIONS & SPICY
CUCUMBERS • PAN-
FRIED OYSTERS WITH
CORNMEAL BREADING &
MEYER LEMON
BUTTER SAUCE

Entrées
LINGUINI WITH PARMA
PROSCIUTTO, ROASTED
SHALLOTS, BABY
TURNIPS & BALSAMIC
VINEGAR CREAM • RACK
OF LAMB WITH MINTED
GREMOLATA & ROASTED
GARLIC GLAZE

PERCHED HIGH ON A HILL OVERLOOKING THE SAUSALITO harbor, the Casa Madrona Restaurant is a romantic reminder of a less hurried time. A narrow brick path, winding by madrones, fragrant pines and an orange tree, leads to what was once a Victorian mansion. ◆ The restaurant retains much of its 1885 charm, but with some welcome modern additions — such as sliding glass walls and a retractable roof over the beautiful outdoor deck. Here, countless men have been driven to propose, intoxicated by the food, the wine and the magnificent view of sea and sky. ◆ Chef Kirke Byers allows flavors to speak for themselves in simple, delightful combinations that soothe rather than startle the palate. The housemade breads and desserts, including chocolate decadence cake worth every bite, complete the recipe for excellence owner John W. Mays has been perfecting for eight years.

AVERAGE DINNER FOR TWO: $65
DOES NOT INCLUDE WINE, TAX AND GRATUITY

GUAYMAS

◆

5 MAIN STREET
AT THE FERRY LANDING
TIBURON, CA 94920
(415) 435-6300

Major Credit Cards
Open Daily • Lunch & Dinner

General Manager
HATCH

Chef
FRANCISCO CISNEROS

Menu Highlights

Appetizers
CORN TORTILLA BOATS
WITH CHICKEN,
JALAPEÑOS, RED ONIONS,
FRESH CHEESE &
SOUR CREAM

Entrées
GIANT SHRIMP
MARINATED IN LIME JUICE
& CILANTRO • POBLANO
CHILES STUFFED WITH
CHICKEN & RAISINS &
TOPPED WITH WALNUT
SAUCE & POMEGRANATE
SEEDS • ROASTED HALF
DUCK WITH PUMPKIN
SEED SAUCE

LIKE THE MEXICAN FISHING VILLAGE IT WAS NAMED AFTER, Guaymas has real South-of-the-Border spirit. Its modern adobe setting, bright colors, outdoor patios and waterfront location make it a popular spot to relax and enjoy the view across the bay. ◆ Chef Francisco Cisneros, a native of Jalisco, Mexico, introduces Americans to the true cuisine of Mexico. The typical burritos and fajitas aren't found here, and no one seems to miss them, either. Instead, fresh seasonal fish is lightly marinated in lime juice, tamales are wrapped in real cornhusks or banana leaves, and homemade tortillas and chips are brought fresh and hot to the table. It's a menu that emphasizes lightness, simplicity and, above all, authenticity. ◆ As you sit back, sip your margarita and look out over the water, it's easy to imagine that you've been transported to the coast of Mexico.

AVERAGE DINNER FOR TWO: $35
DOES NOT INCLUDE WINE, TAX AND GRATUITY

IL FORNAIO

223 TOWN CENTER
CORTE MADERA, CA 94925
(415) 927-4400

MasterCard & Visa Only
Open Daily • Lunch & Dinner • Sat & Sun Brunch

Restaurant Director
BERNARD BREHIER

Chef
MICHAEL POWERS

Menu Highlights

Appetizers
OVEN-ROASTED DOME-SHAPED FOCACCIA WITH SMOKED PROSCIUTTO • GRILLED EGGPLANT, GOAT CHEESE, SUNDRIED TOMATOES, SWEET ONIONS, CAPERS • COLD SEA BASS MARINATED WITH SAGE, JUNIPER BERRIES, BAY LEAF, WINE VINEGAR

Entrées
FREE-RANGE CHICKEN FROM THE ROTISSERIE • THIN BREAD PASTA, SAUSAGE, ONIONS, RED WINE • GRILLED POUNDED VEAL, OLIVE OIL & LEMON

AS YOU APPROACH IL FORNAIO, THE IRRESISTIBLE AROMA OF fresh-baked bread fills the air. Inside, a persimmon ceiling, bottles of imported olive oil and wine, and marble tables surrounded by an animated crowd transform this small corner of Marin into a Tuscan grand cafe. Outside, the heated brick patio with large umbrellas and bubbling fountain heighten the illusion of being in Italy. ◆ Developed by Larry Mindel, who masterminded Ciao, Prego and MacArthur Park, Il Fornaio is a wonderful synthesis of his eye for design and his taste for all things Italian. With the help of Restaurant Director Bernard Brehier, he selected Chef Michael Powers to prepare aromatic trattoria fare from an oakwood-burning pizza oven and rotisserie in the open kitchen. Spit-roasted fowl and game, fish baked in terracotta and daily offerings of risotto and pasta are accompanied by breads served hot from the adjacent bakery. From the espresso cups to the biscotti, everything at Il Fornaio is authentic and satisfying.

AVERAGE DINNER FOR TWO: $35
DOES NOT INCLUDE WINE, TAX AND GRATUITY

JOE LOCOCO'S

◆

300 DRAKES LANDING ROAD
AT SIR FRANCIS DRAKE
GREENBRAE, CA 94904
(415) 925-0808

Major Credit Cards
Open Daily for Dinner • Lunch Mon-Fri

Chef/Proprietor
JOE LOCOCO

Chef
STEVE PAPPAS

Menu Highlights

Appetizers
GRILLED DUCK SAUSAGE
& RADICCHIO WITH
BALSAMIC VINEGAR &
VIRGIN OLIVE OIL •
TUSCAN BRUSCHETTA
WITH FRESH TOMATOES,
OLIVE OIL & OREGANO

Entrées
SNAIL-SHAPED PASTA WITH
TRUFFLES • ZITI WITH
EGGPLANT & RICOTTA •
PRAWNS SAUTÉED WITH
SUNDRIED TOMATOES,
SAFFRON, GARLIC
& HERBS

YOU KNOW YOU'RE ON TO SOMETHING GOOD WHEN YOU leave a restaurant to open another and the entire clientele follows *en masse*. Joe LoCoco is the lucky man blessed with such an appreciative following. Due to its unpretentious ambiance and LoCoco's considerable talents, the restaurant has been a success since its opening in 1987. ◆ LoCoco, raised in Buffalo, spent time in Livorno, Italy, honing his skills in preparing traditional Italian cuisine. He and Chef Steve Pappas use age-old recipes (some dating from medieval times) utilizing fresh vegetables, housemade pasta and wild game to create hearty, peasant-style dishes. ◆ The dining room's peach stucco walls are covered with plates from Siena, paintings from Florence and Tuscan pottery. Large windows open on views of the bay and Mt. Tamalpais. Dining *al fresco* on the outdoor patio is another way to savor the Tuscan experience.

AVERAGE DINNER FOR TWO: $45
DOES NOT INCLUDE WINE, TAX AND GRATUITY

THE LARK CREEK INN

234 MAGNOLIA AVENUE
LARKSPUR, CA 94939
(415) 924-7766

Major Credit Cards
Open Daily for Dinner • Lunch Mon-Fri
Sunday Brunch

Proprietor
MICHAEL DELLAR

Chef
STEPHEN SIMMONS
Chef/Proprietor
BRADLEY OGDEN

Menu Highlights

Appetizers
HERBED FLATBREAD WITH
TOMATOES, EGGPLANT,
DRY-AGED JACK
CHEESE & OLIVE
PESTO • SUMMER
VEGETABLE STEW WITH
LOBSTER & HOMEMADE
EGG NOODLES
Entrées
OVEN-ROASTED SALMON
WITH SPOON CORNBREAD,
BARBECUED PRAWNS &
CHERVIL TOMATO BROTH •
ROTISSERIE OF QUAIL
WITH GRILLED LEEKS &
ROASTED WILD
MUSHROOMS

LIKE AN OLD-FASHIONED NEW ENGLAND COUNTRY RESTAU-
rant, The Lark Creek Inn has a timeless quality that resists trends and
invites relaxation. Bradley Ogden, the former Campton Place executive chef who gave a new luster to American cuisine, and restaurateur
Michael Dellar have put their talents together in what may be the
most refreshing restaurant to open in years. ♦ "We were striving to be
the quintessential American restaurant," says Dellar, " a place that
feels so good locals want to drop in on a regular basis." White walls,
hardwood floors, a creekside patio and a bar with its own late-night
menu are charming not only locals but also every fan of Bradley
Ogden's robustly flavored yet simple cuisine. ♦ Ogden and Chef
Stephen Simmons make everything from scratch, from breads to jams
and pickles. Brunch at The Lark Creek Inn may be the ultimate experience: apple-smoked ham steak with figs and melon and wild berry
flapjacks with Meyer lemon butter are but two of its temptations.

AVERAGE DINNER FOR TWO: $60
DOES NOT INCLUDE WINE, TAX AND GRATUITY

REMILLARD'S

◆

125 EAST SIR FRANCIS DRAKE BOULEVARD
LARKSPUR, CA 94939
(415) 461-3700

Major Credit Cards
Open Daily • Lunch & Dinner

General Manager
T. J. JACOBBERGER

Chef
EMILE WALDTEUFEL

Menu Highlights

Appetizers
FRESH MAINE LOBSTER
WRAPPED IN A CREPE,
NANTUA SAUCE •
MEDALLIONS OF SALMON
& SCALLOP MOUSSE WITH
TOMATO COULIS &
ANGELHAIR PASTA

Entrées
MARINATED RACK OF
LAMB WITH BÉARNAISE
SAUCE • VEAL SWEET-
BREADS WITH BRAISED
ENDIVE • CONFIT OF
DUCK ON A BED OF SAVOY
CABBAGE • FRESH
POACHED SALMON IN
CHIVE SAUCE

SNUG WITHIN THE 1891 GREEN BRAE BRICK KILN BUILT BY Pierre Remillard, Remillard's has a genuine historic feel that makes Emile Waldteufel's classic French cuisine even more enjoyable. Thick curving walls, their bricks fused together by years of heat, surround diners in a softly lit, romantic warmth reminiscent of a wine cellar in France. ◆ When developer Ray Kuratek approached him with the idea of opening a restaurant in the abandoned kiln, Waldteufel, who brought fame to Le Castel in San Francisco during his seven years there, jumped at the chance. Both of them agreed that casual Marinites would welcome formal French cuisine if it was sensibly priced, and they were right. In one year, Remillard's has earned a loyal local following and attracted serious diners from all around the bay. ◆ Known for his perfectionism, Waldteufel adheres to tradition even in his daily specials: a marinated saddle of lamb, for instance, is wrapped in veal mousse and served with truffle sauce. His individual dessert soufflés, from Grand Marnier to mocha, are hailed as the ultimate.

AVERAGE DINNER FOR TWO: $80
DOES NOT INCLUDE WINE, TAX AND GRATUITY

SAVANNAH GRILL

◆

55 TAMAL VISTA
AT MADERA
CORTE MADERA, CA 94925
(415) 924-6774

Major Credit Cards
Open Daily • Lunch & Dinner

Proprietor
KEITH JONES

Chef
NILS EKEROTH

Menu Highlights

Appetizers
CHICKEN SKEWER WITH RED SESAME SALSA & GRILLED SCALLIONS • GULF PRAWNS WITH SPICY RED CURRY CREAM, PEANUTS & PAPAYA

Entrées
GARLIC FETTUCCINI WITH PRAWNS, BAY SCALLOPS, ROMA TOMATOES, ROASTED GARLIC & AGED REGGIANO CHEESE • SKIRT STEAK MARINATED IN BLACK BEAN CHILI SAUCE & BEER

IN MARIN, THE SAVANNAH GRILL IS THE PLACE TO SEE AND BE seen. With a cherrywood and brass decor created by designer Pat Kuleto, the restaurant is made for people-watching, with a long, narrow dining room overlooking a lively bar on one side and an attractive black-hooded open kitchen on the other. ◆ In this upbeat, unpretentious environment, Chef Nils Ekeroth creates cuisine best described as regional American. Ekeroth concentrates on deftly prepared hardwood-grilled and smoked meats and fish, and draws on Asian, Latin and European influences and fresh ingredients to infuse them with intense, distinctive flavors. ◆ Regular patrons definitely have their favorites. "We've tried changing the menu completely, but our customers won't let us," declares Keith Jones. Nevertheless, the bulk of the menu changes every three months, with up to fifteen daily specials spotlighting fresh seafood, salads and pasta dishes.

AVERAGE DINNER FOR TWO: $35
DOES NOT INCLUDE WINE, TAX AND GRATUITY

The legend continues with cream.

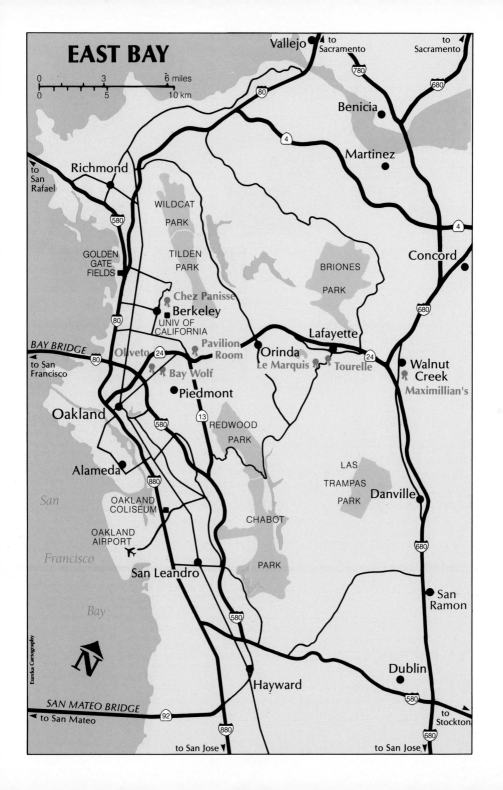

BAY WOLF

◆

3853 PIEDMONT AVENUE
AT RIO VISTA
OAKLAND, CA 94611
(415) 655-6004

MasterCard & Visa Only
Open Daily for Dinner • Lunch Mon-Fri

Proprietor	Chef/Proprietor
LARRY GOLDMAN	**MICHAEL WILD**
Maître d'	*Chef*
MARK McLEOD	**NATHAN PETERSON**

Menu Highlights

Appetizers
GRILLED SCALLOPS WITH
LENTIL SALAD, YELLOW
BEANS & PARSLEY • DUCK
LIVER FLAN WITH FIGS,
PISTACHIOS &
WHITE WINE

Entrées
GRILLED SEA BASS WITH
CITRUS AIOLI, SUMMER
SQUASH GRATIN &
FRISÉE • SAUTÉED
CHICKEN & PRAWNS WITH
HAZELNUTS, CHOCOLATE
& ORANGE • ROASTED
LEG OF LAMB WITH
CHANTERELLES & HERBED
POLENTA CAKE

IT IS REASSURING TO KNOW THAT SINCERE RESTAURANTS ARE still doing well in this inconstant world. Oakland diners have depended upon Michael Wild and Larry Goldman to keep one step ahead of culinary fads for sixteen years, ever since they took a vacant house and transformed it into the sunny, art-filled oasis that is the Bay Wolf today. ◆ Everything here feels *comme il faut* — the awning-covered deck, the gleaming brass espresso machine on the bar, and the friendly faces of the experienced waiters and waitresses. ◆ Lunch or dinner, Bay Wolf continues to delight and satisfy with its innovative and changing menus. Says Michael Wild, "After sixteen years it is still a challenge to keep the food exciting." The restaurant's modest but formidable wine list has become legendary in the wine world.

AVERAGE DINNER FOR TWO: $50
DOES NOT INCLUDE WINE, TAX AND GRATUITY

CHEZ PANISSE
◆

1517 SHATTUCK AVENUE
AT CEDAR
BERKELEY, CA 94701
(415) 548-5525

Major Credit Cards
Closed Sunday & Monday • Dinner Only

Chef/Proprietor
ALICE WATERS

Chef
PAUL BERTOLLI

Menu Highlights

Appetizers
RISOTTO & CORN
TIMBALE WITH LEMONS &
SHRIMP • ROCKFISH &
CRAB SOUP WITH
TOMATOES & BASIL •
GRILLED SCALLIONS &
PEPPERS WITH BAKED
GOAT'S MILK RICOTTA

Entrées
GRILLED DUCK WITH
BAKED FIGS, RED WINE
VINEGAR SAUCE &
MICHAEL'S POTATOES •
SPIT-ROASTED JAMES
RANCH LAMB WITH
MUSTARD SAUCE &
BROWNED POTATOES

FAMED FOR ORIGINALITY, THE UNCOMPROMISING QUALITY of its ingredients and the vision of Alice Waters, Chez Panisse is a great American restaurant with an international reputation. ◆ The free spirit so pervasive in Berkeley also prevails in this kitchen. Since opening in 1971, Chez Panisse has seldom repeated a dish on its prix-fixe menu (currently $55). As the culinary shrine of the American food revolution, it has fresh-produce suppliers knocking on the back door every day. Their produce is organically grown and their meat contains no chemicals. "We're never satisfied," Waters says. "We're always reaching and searching, searching and reaching." ◆ Other culinary heavyweights have cooked here, then gone on to create their own noted kitchens — Jeremiah Tower, Joyce Goldstein and Jean-Pierre Moullé, to name a few. Today, Chef Paul Bertolli shows equal creativity with his own style of seasoning and cooking.

AVERAGE DINNER FOR TWO: $110
DOES NOT INCLUDE WINE, TAX AND GRATUITY

LE MARQUIS

◆

3524B MOUNT DIABLO BOULEVARD
AT FIRST
LAFAYETTE, CA 94549
(415) 284-4422

Major Credit Cards
Closed Sunday & Monday • Dinner Only

Proprietor
SUSAN GUERGUY

Chef/Proprietor
ROBERT GUERGUY

Menu Highlights

Appetizers
SMOKED DUCK
RAVIOLI WITH
GINGER, HONEY &
CABERNET SAUCE •
TERRINE OF GOAT
CHEESE ON A BED OF
BABY LETTUCES

Entrées
GRILLED AHI TUNA
WITH A COMPOTE
OF TOMATO, PEPPERS
& ONIONS • BEEF
TENDERLOIN WITH
A FOUR-PEPPERCORN
& PORT SAUCE •
NOISETTES OF
LAMB RIVIERA

LE MARQUIS WAS ONE OF THE FIRST RESTAURANTS TO SERVE fine cuisine in Contra Costa County. Since Chef Robert Guerguy opened it in 1977, he has won the loyalty of East Bay gourmets with his classic yet light style. ◆ Located in a Lafayette shopping mall, Le Marquis is decorated in soft tones of celadon and peach, with a beautiful contemporary bar and lots of mirrors. An abundance of greenery and fresh flowers in the dining room adds to the pleasant ambiance. ◆ It's a lovely setting for the cuisine of Chef Guerguy, a master saucier who trained on the French Riviera, then spent five years at La Bourgogne and Ernie's in San Francisco. Equal attention is given to the presentation and service by a friendly and professional staff under the direction of hostess Susan Guerguy. Le Marquis also specializes in customized catering for special occasions.

AVERAGE DINNER FOR TWO: $60
DOES NOT INCLUDE WINE, TAX AND GRATUITY

MAXIMILLIAN'S

◆

1604 LOCUST STREET
NEAR BONANZA
WALNUT CREEK, CA 94596
(415) 932-1474

*Major Credit Cards
Closed Sunday • Lunch & Dinner*

Proprietor
MAX WOLFE

Chef
BERNARD MANSARD

Menu Highlights

Appetizers
FRESH SALMON TARTARE ON MARINATED SHAVED FENNEL • SAUTEED SEA SCALLOPS & SPINACH WITH BLACK PEPPER DRESSING • CREAM OF ARTICHOKE SOUP WITH CRUSHED HAZELNUTS

Entrées
PEKING DUCK WITH PLUM SAUCE • FILET OF BEEF WITH ROQUEFORT & CABERNET SAUCE • GRILLED SWORDFISH WITH RED & YELLOW BELL PEPPER SAUCE • RACK OF LAMB

A DINNER AT MAXIMILLIAN'S IN DOWNTOWN WALNUT CREEK can either be California nouvelle or classic French; take your pick. The street-level dining room, decorated in rose and green, has a light, comfortable and upscale feeling. The menu is innovative, featuring California products and an abundance of seafood. A grand-piano player entertains Tuesdays through Saturdays. ◆ The upstairs dining room, oak paneled with old brick touches and dark red carpeting, has a more sedate, traditional ambiance. Here, the cuisine emphasizes classic Continental dishes, and service is more formal. ◆ Proprietor Maximillian Wolfe (Max to his customers) has been in the restaurant industry for twenty-eight years. Chef Bernard Mansard prepares fresh seafood and meat dishes that reflect the influences of France, Japan and California. "Cooking is an art," he says. " I feel it, live it and work to perfect my art. It is my life."

AVERAGE DINNER FOR TWO: $60
DOES NOT INCLUDE WINE, TAX AND GRATUITY

OLIVETO

◆

5655 COLLEGE AVENUE
NEAR BART STATION
OAKLAND, CA 94618
(415) 547-5356

Mastercard & Visa Only
Closed Sunday • Lunch & Dinner

Proprietor
MAGGIE KLEIN

Chef
CURT CLINGMAN

Menu Highlights

Appetizers
RISOTTO WITH CALAMARI,
SHRIMP, TOMATOES &
FRESH THYME •
PERCIATELLI PASTA WITH
ROASTED PEPPERS,
CARAMELIZED ONIONS,
MARJORAM & TOASTED
BREADCRUMBS

Entrées
GRILLED YELLOWFIN TUNA
WITH GRILLED TOMATO,
ROASTED PEPPERS,
TAPENADE & LEMON •
ROASTED VEAL BREAST &
PEPPERONI SAUSAGE WITH
WHITE WINE, ROSEMARY
& TOMATOES

MAGGIE KLEIN'S BOOK, *THE FEAST OF THE OLIVE* (1983), IS A celebration of olive oil and the cuisine of the Mediterranean. The high point of her research, a stay at an eleventh-century Tuscan estate, was the inspiration for her restaurant, Oliveto. ◆ "I wanted my restaurant to evoke a feeling of *la dolce vita*, with an emphasis on grilling, fresh vegetables, salads, stews and good wines," declares Klein. The restaurant and café are reminiscent of a villa in Tuscany, with light terracotta plaster walls and subtle Mediterranean warmth. ◆ The informal downstairs café is a favorite locals' haunt, offering unusual tapas and pizzas. The restaurant upstairs boasts excellent Northern Italian fare, an outstanding wine list of French, Italian, Spanish and domestic vintages, and a gifted chef, Curt Clingman. Clingman draws on his formal classical training, experience in the kitchens of California and travels in Italy to create Oliveto's *cucina rustica*.

AVERAGE DINNER FOR TWO: $50
DOES NOT INCLUDE WINE, TAX AND GRATUITY

PAVILION ROOM

◆

CLAREMONT RESORT HOTEL
ASHBY & DOMINGO AVENUES
OAKLAND, CA 94623
(415) 843-3000

Major Credit Cards
Open Daily • Breakfast, Lunch & Dinner

Food & Beverage Director
WILLIAM SANDER

Corporate Chef
ALAN BARONE

Menu Highlights

Appetizers
SMOKED CARPACCIO OF
BEEF WITH SESAME
TARTARE, SWEET POTATO
CHIPS & WHOLE-GRAIN
CALIFORNIA MUSTARD

Entrées
GRILLED PACIFIC
SWORDFISH WITH
LENTIL-CILANTRO
BROTH, SONOMA JACK
RAVIOLI & PICKLED
WAX BEANS • SAUTÉED
LOIN OF VEAL
WITH CARROT SYRUP,
CORN-CUMIN SAUCE
& CALIFORNIA
CHARD GRATIN

THE ONLY RESORT IN THE BAY AREA, THE CLAREMONT HOTEL is a California landmark, built in 1915 just in time for the Panama-Pacific Exhibition. The venerable hotel commands panoramic views of San Francisco's bay and bridges from its lofty position in the Oakland hills. ◆Over the years, the Claremont has seen many changes. The latest is a full European spa and the premiere of spa cuisine in the Pavilion Room. "Americans have changed their lifestyles," says Food and Beverage Director William Sander. "They're now more health-conscious, so we've made healthful changes in our menu." ◆Chef Alan Barone meets the daily challenges of the Pavilion Room's guests, who are more adventurous concerning cuisine and have high expectations regarding service. "Our produce and fish are hand-selected from local markets," says Barone, "and we harvest our herbs daily from the restaurant's private garden."

AVERAGE DINNER FOR TWO: $70
DOES NOT INCLUDE WINE, TAX AND GRATUITY

TOURELLE

◆

3565 Mt. Diablo Boulevard
AT OAK HILL
Lafayette, Ca 94549
(415) 284-3565

Major Credit Cards
Open Daily • Lunch & Dinner • Sunday Brunch

Manager
LANCE BELLAMY

Chef
STEPHEN SILVA

Menu Highlights

Appetizers
BAKED POLENTA WITH
GOAT CHEESE &
ROASTED GARLIC
SERVED WITH ITALIAN
FLATBREAD • FISH STEW
BASQUAISE WITH
PRAWNS & MUSSELS

Entrées
DUCK CONFIT SALAD
WITH RASPBERRY WALNUT
VINAIGRETTE • HOUSE-
SMOKED PORK CHOP
WITH SPICY APRICOT
COMPOTE • PIZZA WITH
SMOKED LAMB SAUSAGE,
SWEET PEPPERS
& FONTINA

WITH A WALK DOWN A FLAGSTONE PATH PAST FRAGRANT herb and flower gardens, Tourelle transports you to the South of France. The historic vine-covered chateau retains the original brick tower from which Tourelle ("little tower") gets its name. ◆ One of the most romantic restaurants in the Bay Area, Tourelle has a timeless, European ambiance. The high vaulted ceilings, pine floors and clean-lined furniture are reminiscent of a French farmhouse — an ideal backdrop for Chef Stephen Silva's country European cuisine. A graduate of the Culinary Institute of America in Hyde Park, New York, he blends Italian and French flavors in direct, uncomplicated dishes. ◆ The lively exhibition kitchen, redesigned by Pat Kuleto, is visible from all dining rooms, and live jazz fills the air.

AVERAGE DINNER FOR TWO: $50
DOES NOT INCLUDE WINE, TAX AND GRATUITY

Omelettes aux tomates, pain au chocolat,

omelettes aux fromages, baguettes, butter brioche, omelettes aux champignons, jambon, pommes rissolées, pommes frites, bananas, oranges, apples, papaya, mangos, peaches, pears, cantaloupe, honeydew, pineapple, sausage, bacon, ham, blueberry, strawberry, cranberry and almond muffins, blueberry pancakes, pain au raisin, Swiss, Edam and cottage cheese, Brie, Camembert, crêpes, Belgian waffles, cereal, oatmeal, oeufs Benedictines, French toast, café au lait, hot chocolate, freshly squeezed orange juice, mineral water, spring water, Earl Grey, chamomile, peppermint and herbal tea, and pots of assorted jams.

[And that's only *breakfast*.]

This morning, on dozens of sunswept terraces overlooking dozens of sparkling bays, some very relaxed people are having fresh juice, and anything else they want. After playing in turquoise waters all morning, they'll return for a lunch of French breads, cheeses, salads, grilled chicken and wine. Later, they'll sip creamy piña coladas on a sugar-sand beach. Then, toward sunset, corks will pop, and the sweet aromas of veal Marsala, swordfish, soufflés and ocean breezes will mark the opening of a continental restaurant. For reservations, simply phone your travel agent or 1-800-CLUB MED®

Club Med
The antidote for civilization.

THE GRANDEST MARNIER.

Grand Marnier Cent cinquantenaire, an exquisite blend of specially aged cognac with a distinctive hint of wild oranges, was created to commemorate the 150th anniversary of Grand Marnier. Available in a very limited edition. It is the quintessential gift.

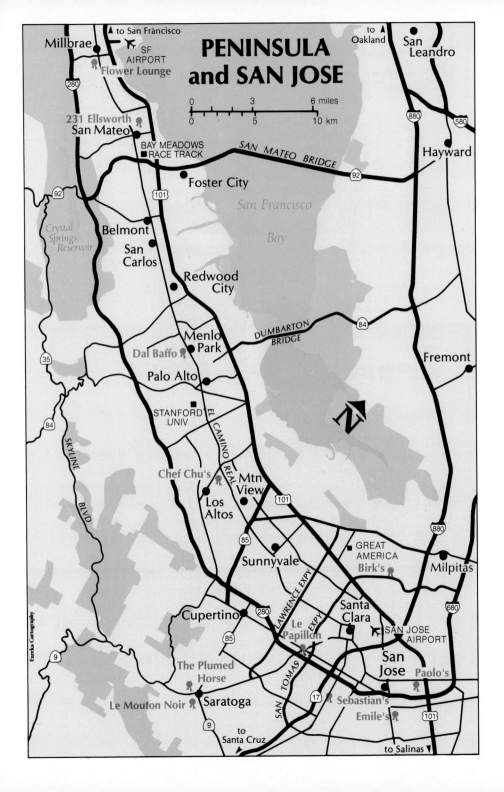

BIRK'S

◆

3955 FREEDOM CIRCLE
AT HWY 101 & GREAT AMERICA PKWY
SANTA CLARA, CA 95054
(408) 980-6400

Major Credit Cards
Open Daily for Dinner • Lunch Mon-Fri

Proprietors
JIM SCHLOSS
DON DURANTE

Chef
JIM STUMP

Menu Highlights

Appetizers
GRILLED SEAFOOD
SAUSAGE WITH HONEY
MUSTARD • MEXICAN
SHRIMP SAUTÉ WITH
CRACKED PEPPER, CRISP-
FRIED GARLIC & LIME •
SOUTHERN-STYLE
CRABCAKES WITH SHERRY
MUSTARD SAUCE

Entrées
DRY-AGED NEW YORK
STEAK BROILED OVER RED
OAK • BROILED CENTER-
CUT PORK CHOPS •
SMOKED PRIME RIB WITH
ONION BREAD PUDDING &
CREAMED SPINACH

A JOINT EFFORT BY BIRK MCCANDLESS, JIM SCHLOSS AND DON Durante, Birk's is a sophisticated American grill designed by Pat Kuleto. Lodged in a futuristic building beneath the first of two proposed McCandless towers, it is the place where the Silicon Valley comes to unwind. ◆ A long mahogany bar faces the entrance, with three brass standards that dispense eighteen draft beers. Behind the bar, open shelves loaded with premium spirits reach to a redwood-beamed ceiling. Multilevel dining areas provide a choice of deep booths and private tables or counter seating by an open-to-view kitchen. ◆ "We do food America loves and people will come back to," says Jim Schloss. Conceived by Durante, owner of Le Mouton Noir in Saratoga, the traditional menu of grilled and smoked meat, fish and fowl is brought to life by Chef Jim Stump, who perfected his skills with Hubert Keller at Fleur de Lys and Patrizio Sacchetto at The Blue Fox.

AVERAGE DINNER FOR TWO: $60
DOES NOT INCLUDE WINE, TAX AND GRATUITY

CHEF CHU'S

◆

1067 NORTH SAN ANTONIO ROAD
AT EL CAMINO REAL
LOS ALTOS, CA 94022
(415) 948-2696

Major Credit Cards
Open Daily • Lunch & Dinner

Manager
CHARLIE ONG

Chef/Proprietor
LAWRENCE CHU

Menu Highlights

Appetizers
CATFISH ROLL •
CRISPY-FRIED SHRIMP
BALLS • MINCED
CHICKEN •
POTSTICKERS •
SMOKED FISH
SHANGHAI-STYLE

Entrées
PEKING DUCK •
SZECHUAN-STYLE
DRY BRAISED
PRAWNS • MU SHU
PORK • PRAWNS WITH
CANDIED PECANS IN
LIGHT MUSTARD SAUCE
• BRAISED WHOLE
FRESH FISH

CHEF CHU'S, LOCATED IN THE HEART OF THE PENINSULA'S EL Camino Real nightlife, is celebrating its twentieth anniversary and entering the 1990s with Chinese cuisine that reflects a new era of fresh, nutritious and unpretentious food. In the downstairs bar and dining room, the mood is bustling, upbeat and fun. The upstairs dining room is more formal, with a magnificent wood carving of the Nine Dragons covering an entire wall. ◆ Author of the bestselling cookbook *Chef Chu's Distinctive Cuisine of China*, Chef Lawrence Chu is the guiding force behind this restaurant. "To enjoy food," says Chu, "you must be relaxed, in a good mood and in the proper atmosphere." ◆ Chu's spirit is everywhere; he can be seen in the spotless kitchen preparing Lover's Prawns for newlyweds or in the lobby, scrawling a Chinese birthday greeting on the signboard for an 86-year-old guest. Chef Chu is frequently seen on television sharing his wok cooking skills, and is more than happy to advise his patrons in menu planning.

AVERAGE DINNER FOR TWO: $30
DOES NOT INCLUDE WINE, TAX AND GRATUITY

DAL BAFFO

◆

878 SANTA CRUZ AVENUE
AT UNIVERSITY DRIVE
MENLO PARK, CA 94025
(415) 325-1588

Major Credit Cards
Closed Sunday • Lunch & Dinner

☎ 🍸 🍴 🎥 PR

Chef/Proprietor
VINCENZO LOGRASSO

Chef de Cuisine
ANDRÉ GUERGUY
Executive Chef
CHRISTIAN ISER

Menu Highlights

Appetizers
MIXED MUSHROOMS
SAUTÉED WITH HERBS &
SOURDOUGH TOAST •
FRESH ARTICHOKES A LA
ROMANA • PETITE
BOUCHÉE OF BAY
SCALLOPS WITH
CHAMPAGNE SAUCE &
SPRING VEGETABLES

Entrées
BROILED OR POACHED
SALMON FILET WITH
SUNDRIED TOMATOES &
TARRAGON HOLLANDAISE •
MEDALLIONS OF BEEF
WITH FOIE GRAS & BLACK
TRUFFLE SAUCE

CHEF VINCENZO LOGRASSO IS PROUD OF HIS ELEGANT restaurant, opened in 1977 near Stanford University in Menlo Park. Trained at the Culinary Academy of Genoa, Italy, LoGrasso is assisted in the kitchen by Chef de Cuisine André Guerguy and Executive Chef Christian Iser. ◆ Sicilian pastas are an important part of the menu, but Genovese, French and Californian influences are also represented. The ten to twelve specials offered each day reflect an emphatically fresh, original style. LoGrasso also creates one or two low-calorie entrées daily for his health-conscious patrons. ◆ A spacious bar and lounge area, perfect for a before-dinner wine or an after-dinner espresso, features wood paneling and comfortable lounge chairs. Behind etched-glass doors is a beautifully remodeled banquet room that seats up to forty people. The extraordinary wine list, with exceptional varietals from California, France, Italy, Spain and Germany, has been the recipient of *The Wine Spectator* Grand Award since 1985.

AVERAGE DINNER FOR TWO: $70
DOES NOT INCLUDE WINE, TAX AND GRATUITY

EMILE'S

◆

545 SOUTH SECOND STREET
SAN JOSE, CA 95112
(408) 289-1960

Major Credit Cards
Dinner Tues-Sat • Lunch Tues-Fri

Manager
CHRISTINE MOOSER

Chef
JAMES CONNOLLY
Chef/Proprietor
EMILE MOOSER

Menu Highlights

Appetizers
HOUSE-CURED SALMON
WITH YOGURT &
DILL SAUCE •
CRAB & FISH CAKES
WITH RED BELL
PEPPER COULIS &
SEASONAL GREENS

Entrées
ROASTED RACK OF
LAMB SERVED ON A
BED OF RATATOUILLE •
ROASTED LOIN OF
PORK, COUNTRY
STYLE, WITH GARLIC
PUREED POTATOES
& FRESH SEASONAL
FRUIT COMPOTE

CHEF EMILE MOOSER, TRAINED IN CLASSIC OLD-WORLD style in Lausanne, Switzerland, is mentor to numerous aspiring cooks. Emile's, known affectionately in the South Bay as a "mother restaurant," is the leader of the restaurant industry here, celebrating its nineteenth year. ◆ Emile is noted for his detailed attention to seasoning, color and shapes in presentation and to texture of sauces. "My formal training in the wine country above Lake Geneva taught me the intricacies of the proper marriage of food and wine," says Emile. His managerial skills ensure meticulous service. ◆ Although committed to high standards, he is versatile as well, changing the menu bi-monthly. Chef James Connolly has worked closely with Emile for ten years to keep the quality consistent. The off-white walls, white linen and upholstered cane chairs provide an intimate, plush setting that highlights the cuisine.

AVERAGE DINNER FOR TWO: $60
DOES NOT INCLUDE WINE, TAX AND GRATUITY

FLOWER LOUNGE

◆

51 MILLBRAE AVENUE
AT EL CAMINO REAL
MILLBRAE, CA 94030
(415) 692-6666

Major Credit Cards
Open Daily • Lunch & Dinner

Proprietor	Chef
ALICE WONG	PHILIP LO

Menu Highlights

Appetizers
SHREDDED DUCK WITH
FRESH FRUITS • CHICKEN
SALAD RAINBOW • FRIED
SEAFOOD WITH CRISPY
NEST • SQUAB BRAISED
IN BEER

Entrées
FRIED PRAWNS WITH
GLAZED WALNUTS IN
SPECIAL SAUCE • BAKED
CRAB HUNAN-STYLE •
BRAISED TOFU WITH
MINCED SHRIMP •
SHREDDED BEEF IN BLACK
PEPPER SAUCE WITH
GREEN ONIONS • SQUAB
WITH MANGO

WHEN ALICE WONG FIRST CAME TO THE BAY AREA TO STUDY economics at Mills College, she expected to join her family's garment business after graduation. Upon her return to Hong Kong, however, she found her family had started a successful chain of celebrated restaurants called Flower Lounge. That was all it took to change her plans. ◆ An ambitious woman, Wong set out to change the American conception of Cantonese food as bland, with little to offer besides unexciting egg rolls and chop suey. She returned to the Bay Area to open the first Flower Lounge outside Hong Kong. ◆ Wong brought Chef Philip Lo back with her to create the subtly spiced, seafood-dominant dishes that are the trademarks of authentic Cantonese haute cuisine. "We spend more time on preparation and less on actual cooking, so that the natural flavors of the ingredients are retained, not masked," says Wong.

AVERAGE DINNER FOR TWO: $30
DOES NOT INCLUDE WINE, TAX AND GRATUITY

LE MOUTON NOIR

◆

14560 BIG BASIN WAY
NEAR HIGHWAY NINE
SARATOGA, CA 95070
(408) 867-7017

Major Credit Cards
Open Daily for Dinner • Lunch Tues-Sat

Proprietor	*Chef*
DON DURANTE	BRIAN WESELBY

Menu Highlights

Appetizers
RED PEPPER PANCAKES
WITH SMOKED SALMON
IN A LIGHT SWEET
CORN SAUCE •
SCALLOP, BELGIAN
ENDIVE & ASPARAGUS
SALAD WITH LIME &
GINGER
VINAIGRETTE

Entrées
DUCK À LA MOUTON
NOIR • ROASTED RACK
OF LAMB SERVED WITH
ROSEMARY & ROASTED
GARLIC SAUCE

CONTRARY TO WHAT ITS NAME IMPLIES, LE MOUTON NOIR IS certainly not "the black sheep" of Saratoga's famous restaurant row. Located in a historic 125-year-old Victorian decorated with Laura Ashley prints, colorful sprays of flowers and tones of pink and dusty rose, this dining establishment has the cheerfulness of a country home. Le Mouton Noir is a favorite with local restaurant connoisseurs. ◆ Proprietor Don Durante and Chef Brian Weselby, trained in England and the South of France, plan the seasonal menus together and rely on local producers for most of their fish, vegetables and herbs. ◆ "It's French-inspired California cuisine," says Durante. "We try to be very progressive, very innovative." Huff's *à la minute* preparation technique captures the full flavor of the fresh seafood, vegetables, beef and prime lamb.

AVERAGE DINNER FOR TWO: $65
DOES NOT INCLUDE WINE, TAX AND GRATUITY

LE PAPILLON

◆

410 SARATOGA AVENUE
AT KIELY
SAN JOSE, CA 95129
(408) 296-3730

Major Credit Cards
Closed Sunday • Lunch & Dinner

☎ 🍸 🚗 🍴 ⛱ PR

Proprietor   *Chef*
MIKE MASHAYEKH   **SCOTT COOPER**

Menu Highlights

Appetizers
BROILED SCALLOPS
A LA LOUISIANE •
HERBED PATÉ •
TORTELLINI WITH
THREE-CHEESE
SAUCE

Entrées
VENISON GRENADINE •
CURRIED PRAWNS •
MEDALLIONS OF
BEEF PARISIEN •
PEPPER STEAK
FLAMBÉ • VEAL
CHAMPIGNONS • BREAST
OF PARTRIDGE IN
RED CURRANT SAUCE

WHEN MIKE MASHAYEKH OPENED LE PAPILLON IN 1977, HE knew that for an executive, the choice of restaurant can be the key to closing a successful deal. His fashionable San Jose establishment is now a favorite spot for local business people, who entertain clients there in a tony atmosphere that appeals to pleasure-seekers as well. The soft lighting, French doors, original French prints, mounted butterflies, flowers and greenery all reflect a thoughtful designer's touch. ◆When the artistry of Chef Scott Cooper goes to work on the taste buds, business becomes the last thing on one's mind. His creativity is most apparent in the light and fresh sauces he prepares daily to enhance fresh fish, poultry and meat dishes. Savor this list: thyme-horseradish, pomegranate, raspberry beurre blanc, thistle-honey orange. Le Papillon means butterfly, a very appropriate image for the brilliance of Cooper's creations.

AVERAGE DINNER FOR TWO: $60
DOES NOT INCLUDE WINE, TAX AND GRATUITY

PAOLO'S

◆

520 EAST SANTA CLARA
AT TWELFTH STREET
SAN JOSE, CA 95112
(408) 294-2558

Major Credit Cards
Dinner Mon-Sat • Lunch Mon-Fri

Maître d'
JALIL SAMAVARCHIAN
Proprietor
JENNY GRIESBACH

Proprietor
CAROLYN ALLEN
Chef
CLYDE GRIESBACH

Menu Highlights

Appetizers
POACHED PRAWNS WITH
TUSCAN WHITE BEAN &
VEGETABLE COMPOTE •
CARPACCIO WITH
SHIITAKE MUSHROOMS &
TRUFFLE-FLAVORED
OLIVE OIL

Entrées
FILET OF SALMON WITH
PURÉE OF FENNEL &
OLIVE OIL • GRILLED
VEAL CHOP WITH
RADICCHIO & FOREST
MUSHROOMS • BRAISED
CHICKEN WITH SPICY RED
PEPPERS, TOMATO &
POLENTA

FOR OVER FORTY ILLUSTRIOUS YEARS, PAOLO'S WAS GUIDED by Jack Allen, a leader in innovative dining in the Santa Clara Valley. Today, Allen's daughters Carolyn Allen and Jenny Griesbach, with Maître d' Jalil Samavarchian and Chef Clyde Griesbach, are guiding the restaurant into a whole new era. ◆ From the diverse wine list, which boasts over 450 Californian and imported selections, to the extensively researched regional Italian cuisine, Paolo's is in capable hands. Chef Clyde Griesbach insists on authenticity, traveling to Sardinia, Tuscany and Piedmont to find treasured regional recipes. His presentation, straightforward yet elegant, reflects a simple contemporary artistry. ◆ "We'll maintain Paolo's traditions," Allen says, "but we've established something new, something that is the direct voice of the second generation." Watch for Paolo's newest revision: a move to a new location in the near future.

AVERAGE DINNER FOR TWO: $60
DOES NOT INCLUDE WINE, TAX AND GRATUITY

THE PLUMED HORSE

◆

14555 BIG BASIN WAY
AT HIGHWAY NINE
SARATOGA, CA 95070
(408) 867-4711

Major Credit Cards
Closed Sunday • Lunch & Dinner

Proprietors
YVONNE & KLAUS PACHE

Chef
THOMAS CRUMPTON

Menu Highlights

Appetizers
BAKED BRIE IN
BRIOCHE WITH GARLIC
SAUCE • ESCARGOTS
WITH GARLIC,
MUSHROOMS, WHITE
WINE, TOMATO &
HERBES DE PROVENCE

Entrées
YOUNG SONOMA RACK OF
LAMB, MARINATED,
ROASTED & SERVED WITH
SAUTÉED GARLIC CLOVES •
ROASTED SQUAB & BLACK
PEPPER LINGUINI,
SAUTÉED WITH ONION,
BACON, WHITE WINE &
WILD MUSHROOMS

THE PICTURESQUE YET SOPHISTICATED TOWN OF SARATOGA is in a historic lumber-and-wine-producing area on the edge of the verdant Santa Cruz Mountains. The Plumed Horse, a mix of Victorian and American styles, sets its own vintage tone. ◆ Proprietors Klaus and Yvonne Pache give each diner all the care and attention they would lavish on any guest in their home. Chef Thomas Crumpton, who trained with Sebastian Urbain of the Pierre at Le Meridien in San Francisco, shares the Paches' dedication. A California native, he began cooking professionally at age 16 and his seasonally changing menu reflects a unique blend of creativity and technique. His dishes also reveal a commitment to the traditional values of the Plumed Horse's thirty-five year history in the Santa Clara Valley. ◆ The colorful, lively Crazy Horse Lounge offers grand piano entertainment and live music for dancing on the weekends. An exceptional wine list earned The Plumed Horse *The Wine Spectator* Grand Award.

AVERAGE DINNER FOR TWO: $75
DOES NOT INCLUDE WINE, TAX AND GRATUITY

SEBASTIAN'S

◆

1901 SOUTH BASCOM AVENUE
AT HAMILTON
CAMPBELL, CA 95008
(408) 377-8600

Major Credit Cards
Open Daily for Dinner • Lunch Mon-Fri

General Manager
GAVIN GRACEY

Chef
ROBERTA COKER

Menu Highlights

Appetizers
SNAILS FLAMED IN
BRANDY WITH GARLIC,
HERBS & CREAM IN
PASTRY SHELL • GRILLED
ARTICHOKES, MARINATED
PEPPERS, ROASTED
EGGPLANT, FETA CHEESE,
NIÇOISE OLIVES

Entrées
ROASTED BREAST OF
PHEASANT WITH D'ANJOU
PEAR & MORELS •
PORCINI MUSHROOMS,
SUNDRIED TOMATOES,
GARLIC & PANCETTA •
GRILLED FILET MIGNON
WITH TRUFFLE SAUCE

FROM THE SEVENTEENTH FLOOR OF THE PRUNEYARD
Towers, the tallest building between San Francisco and Los Angeles,
Sebastian's has built its reputation on exquisitely prepared French and
Italian cuisine, and, not incidentally, on its panoramic views of the
Silicon Valley. "San Jose is going through fast and furious changes,"
says manager Gavin Gracey, "and I'm proud that Sebastian's is one of
the leaders." ◆ Chef Roberta Coker presents extraordinarily colorful
dishes, sometimes including four or five vegetables of different hues
topped with a rainbow of edible flowers. Her menu combines
Mediterranean, Greek and Basque flavors. ◆ The elegant restaurant's
romantic lighting and views of twinkling city lights make it a favorite
destination for lovers. On weekends, guests can enjoy dancing
upstairs at Sebastian's club, Jennie's.

AVERAGE DINNER FOR TWO: $70
DOES NOT INCLUDE WINE, TAX AND GRATUITY

231 ELLSWORTH

◆

231 SOUTH ELLSWORTH STREET
AT THIRD AVENUE
SAN MATEO, CA 94401
(415) 347-7231

Major Credit Cards
Dinner Mon-Sat • Lunch Mon-Fri

| *Proprietor* | *Chef/Proprietor* |
| KEN OTTOBONI | KURT GRASING |

Menu Highlights

Appetizers
SMOKED SALMON WITH
TERRINE OF AVOCADO •
SAUTÉED SCALLOPS WITH
PASSIONFRUIT & GRAINS
OF CAVIAR • SUMMER
SALAD WITH GREEN BEANS,
DUCK ASPIC & DUCK
CONFIT

Entrées
MEDALLIONS OF VENISON
WITH CORN & WHITE
BEANS • SEARED AHI WITH
ROASTED EGGPLANT &
BASIL • BREAST OF DUCK
WITH RASPBERRIES &
BITTERSWEET CHOCOLATE

IN 1988, THE TWO-YEAR-OLD 231 ELLSWORTH EMERGED OUT of nowhere to win the *San Francisco Focus* People's Choice Award for the Peninsula's best French restaurant. Behind this "instant" success, however, were thirteen years of planning, begun when Ken Ottoboni and Kurt Grasing met at San Francisco's Clift Hotel. ◆ Ottoboni spent the years working toward his "lifetime dream" at such restaurants as Le Castel and Fleur de Lys, while Grasing honed his skills at Narsai's, New York's Pierre Hotel and London's only three-star restaurant, Le Gavroche. Together, they have earned a well-deserved place in the spotlight with fresh, modern versions of French cuisine and a well-chosen collection of 300 French and California wines in every price range. ◆ 231 Ellsworth features a seasonal à la carte menu, a four-course, prix-fixe menu and sensational desserts by Pastry Chef Phil Ogiela. No wonder it's the people's choice.

AVERAGE DINNER FOR TWO: $60
DOES NOT INCLUDE WINE, TAX AND GRATUITY

GET THE VIP TREATMENT
YOU DESERVE

CALL

RENDEZVOUS

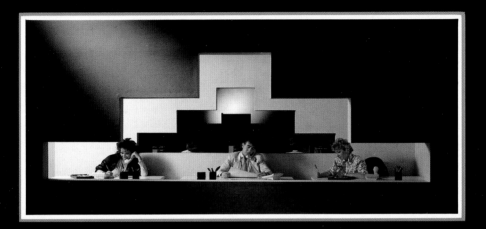

RESERVATIONS

Restaurant Information and Reservation Service.
Person-to-person details on
Northern California's outstanding restaurants.
Type of cuisine...Ambiance...Location...Special Occasions

ALL IN ONE CALL AND ABSOLUTELY FREE!
10:00am-6:00pm Monday through Friday
(415) 777-2676

You must be joking.
Kentucky Champagne?

He was a food and wine critic, a travel magazine editor, basically one of the nation's leading arbiters of good taste. And I had the honor of showing him around Kentucky for a few days.

One of our excursions was to our little distillery near Loretto, where I explained some of the virtues of our whisky that so many Kentuckians seem to prefer. Like a true critic, he politely congratulated us on our efforts in making a quality bourbon, and on the modest success we seem to be having.

Later, we arrived at Stanley Demos' Coach House restaurant in Lexington for dinner. Before anyone working there recognized me, the waiter came to our table and asked if he could bring us something to drink.

That's when my companion did something unusual. He asked the waiter to bring us some "Kentucky Champagne."

I thought, "You must be joking. Kentucky Champagne?"

Then we watched as the waiter went to the bar and asked for Maker's Mark in two brandy snifters.

My friend's genius finally dawned on me. He had tested what I'd told him about the esteem our whisky enjoys in Kentucky. What better way to do it than with one simple metaphor for good taste? With an open-ended request with any number of possible outcomes?

Fortunately, the joke wasn't on me. What if our waiter had come back with something other than Maker's Mark?

He deserved a tip even larger than the one I left.

Bill Samuels, Jr.

Bill Samuels, Jr.
President
Maker's Mark Distillery

Maker's
⑤IV Mark®

Maker's Mark Distillery, Loretto, KY 40037.
45% Alc./Vol. (90Proof), Fully Matured

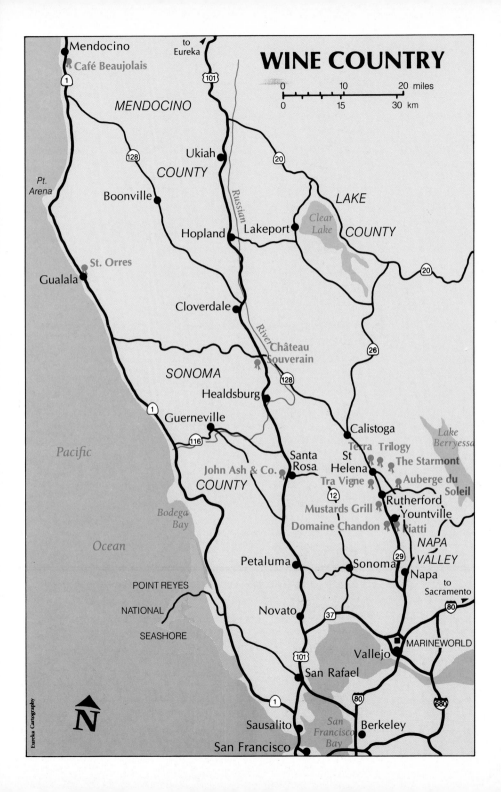

The Spirit Of France

AUBERGE DU SOLEIL

◆

180 RUTHERFORD HILL ROAD
RUTHERFORD, CA 94573
(707) 963-1211

MasterCard & Visa Only
Open Daily • Lunch & Dinner

General Manager
GEORGE A. GOEGGEL

Chef
UDO NECHUTNYS

Menu Highlights

Appetizers
STEAMED SABLE FISH
WITH GREEN LENTILS
& HERBED OLIVE OIL •
SAUTÉED SONOMA
FOIE GRAS WITH
RASPBERRY
VINAIGRETTE

Entrées
DRY-AGED NEW YORK
STEAK, WITH
RATATOUILLE &
GRATIN DAUPHINOIS •
CRISPY PEKING
DUCKLING ON
MESCLUN GREENS
WITH PAPAYA

AUBERGE DU SOLEIL IS A STRIKING SERIES OF JUXTAPOSI-
tions. Earthy stone and wood floors, rough-timber ceilings and cedar
columns are pure Santa Fe, while the French doors, pink tableclothes
and marble table with a bouquet of wild flowers are thoroughly
Provençal. Then there's the deck. Fifteen tables overlook the glorious
Napa Valley, a 160-degree panorama of olive groves, terraced vineyards and rolling foothills, which, when late afternoon turns amber,
could easily be the golden hills of Tuscany. ◆ Executive Chef Udo
Nechutnys's international experience has inspired an equally enchanting mix of contrasts. His French, Oriental and California cuisine
results from years spent in the kitchen of Maxim's in Paris, at the
Mandarin Hotel in Hong Kong and with the renowned Paul Bocuse
in Japan. A decade in California, at Domaine Chandon and the
Miramonte, raised his culinary health consciousness. Says Co-
Proprietor Claude Rouas, "The marriage of Chef Nechutnys and
Auberge du Soleil is a successful one." An understatement, to be sure.

AVERAGE DINNER FOR TWO: $104
DOES NOT INCLUDE WINE, TAX AND GRATUITY

CAFÉ BEAUJOLAIS
◆

961 UKIAH STREET
NEAR EVERGREEN
MENDOCINO, CA 95460
(707) 937-5614

No Credit Cards Accepted
Dinner Thurs-Sun • Breakfast & Lunch Daily

Chef/Proprietor
MARGARET FOX

Chef
CHRISTOPHER KUMP

Menu Highlights

Appetizers
SMOKED CORN &
CHILE SOUP WITH
TORTILLA CHIPS • OXTAIL
& MOREL MUSHROOM
RAVIOLI WITH PORT
& OXTAIL SAUCE

Entrées
STEAMED FRESH
KING SALMON, WITH
FRESH DILL SABAYON
SAUCE & THREE-
GRAIN PILAF •
OSSO BUCCO MADE
WITH FREE-RANGE
VEAL, SERVED WITH
GREMOLATA &
SOFT POLENTA

MENDOCINO HAS LONG BEEN KNOWN AS AN INNOVATIVE artists' colony and as a picturesque, cool coastal retreat. Now it is also known as a haven for gourmets, thanks to Margaret Fox and her Café Beaujolais. ◆ Located on a side street in a 1910 Victorian, Café Beaujolais was first heralded for its astonishing breakfasts, brunches and lunches. "I love breakfast," Fox says. "It's the forgotten meal, and yet people are so appreciative when they have one that is outstanding." ◆ Recently, Fox and Chef Kump have been placing equal emphasis on the à la carte dinners available Thursday through Sunday from April to December. Specialties of the house feature local produce and seafood prepared with an eclectic American and French style. ◆ Chef Fox markets her Panforte de Mendocino and Beaujolais Fruitcake, so visitors can now take a little bit of Mendocino home. The list of California wines changes frequently to include new releases and select vintages.

AVERAGE DINNER FOR TWO: $75
DOES NOT INCLUDE WINE, TAX AND GRATUITY

CHATEAU SOUVERAIN

◆

400 SOUVERAIN ROAD
AT INDEPENDENCE LANE
GEYSERVILLE, CA 95441
(707) 433-3141

Major Credit Cards
Dinner Thurs-Sat • Lunch Tues-Sat • Sunday Brunch

Manager
JANEANNE HARROD

Sous Chef
LANCE VELASQUEZ

Menu Highlights

Appetizers
WARM SALAD OF
SCALLOPS, ROCK SHRIMP
& SPINACH WITH
AVOCADO, GINGER,
MANGO & SESAME

Entrées
OPEN-FACE SMOKED
CHICKEN RAVIOLI
WITH RICOTTA, BRAISED
LEEKS & CHIVES •
SONOMA LAMB
NOISETTES WITH
MUSTARD, PISTACHIOS,
ARTICHOKES, EGGPLANT-
FENNEL COMPOTE &
BASIL-LAMB ESSENCE

THE VIEW FROM THE RESTAURANT AT CHATEAU SOUVERAIN has always been one of the most spectacular in the wine country. Majestically set atop a vine-covered knoll, the restaurant has two windowed "walls" and a large outdoor terrace overlooking the gentle slopes of Sonoma's Alexander Valley. The main dining room with large fireplace and cathedral ceilings opens onto the terrace. ◆Located in the heart of Sonoma wine country, Château Souverain takes advantage of the area's wealth of vegetables, cheeses and meats. Dishes consist of superb flavor and texture combinations, making every meal a classic dining experience. ◆One of the few premium California wineries to offer year-round gourmet dining, Château Souverain has garnered national recognition in such publications as *Food & Wine*, *Gourmet* and *The Wine Spectator*.

AVERAGE DINNER FOR TWO: $65
DOES NOT INCLUDE WINE, TAX AND GRATUITY

DOMAINE CHANDON

◆

CALIFORNIA DRIVE
AT HIGHWAY 29
YOUNTVILLE, CA 94599
(707) 944-2892

Major Credit Cards
Closed Monday & Tuesday • Lunch & Dinner

Manager
DANIEL SHANKS

Chef
PHILIPPE JEANTY

Menu Highlights

Appetizers
HOME-SMOKED
SALMON CARPACCIO •
HOME-SMOKED RED
TROUT SALAD •
SUMMER GARDEN
"TARTE TATIN"

Entrées
SEARED TUNA PEPPER
STEAK WITH GARLIC
POTATO PURÉE &
LEEK RINGS •
SWEETBREAD
MILLEFEUILLE WITH
SHALLOT-TRUFFLE
BUTTER • SONOMA
FARM SPRING LAMB
COOKED THREE WAYS

WHEN THE GREAT HOUSE OF CHAMPAGNE, MOET ET Chandon, came to the United States and established Domaine Chandon in the high-profile Napa Valley, oenophiles expected a great American sparkling wine, and they have not been disappointed. They got even more than they bargained for: a fine French restaurant. ◆ Chef Philippe Jeanty of Epernay, France, trained at the Reims Culinary Academy in the heart of Champagne, was appointed Chef de Cuisine at Domaine Chandon in 1978. "I style my cuisine to reflect California's openness to innovation," he says, "the readily available fresh products and the great traditions of French cooking. And," he adds with a sparkle in his eyes, "I emphasize foods compatible with Champagne." ◆ Manager and Maître d' Daniel Shanks maintains Moët et Chandon's 400-year tradition of hospitality, presenting the cuisine with professional flair but without unnecessary flourish.

AVERAGE DINNER FOR TWO: $90
DOES NOT INCLUDE WINE, TAX AND GRATUITY

JOHN ASH & CO.

◆

4330 BARNES ROAD
NEAR RIVER ROAD
SANTA ROSA, CA 95403
(707) 527-7687

Major Credit Cards
Closed Monday • Lunch & Dinner

☎ 🍸 📷 🍴 🍷 ⛅ ⑤ ∅

Managing Partner
JOHN P. DUFFY

Executive Chef
JOHN ASH

Menu Highlights

Appetizers
SONOMA GAZPACHO •
RILLETTE OF DUCK •
GRAVLAX OF LOCAL
KING SALMON • SALAD
OF FRESH MOZZARELLA
& SUMMER TOMATOES

Entrées
FRESH FISH FROM
AROUND THE
WORLD • MUSCOVY
DUCK • LOIN OF
LAMB WITH
HAZELNUTS, HONEY &
THYME • NEW-YORK
STEAK WITH JACK
DANIEL'S SAUCE

SINCE HE OPENED HIS RESTAURANT IN 1980, JOHN ASH HAS been dubbed "one of the twenty-five hot new chefs in America" by *Food & Wine* magazine. This accolade echoes the sentiments of diners who have savored Ash's cooking. Ash responds to the lavish praise with modesty: "I'm just a refugee from the corporate world." ◆ His cuisine, however, says otherwise. Consistently artistic and inspired, it features the freshest bounty from Sonoma's boutique farms and innovatively revised recipes from all over the world. "America is a mix of all peoples; my food is the same," he says. "California cuisine means using flavors and techniques from various ethnic recipes to create food that is fun, different and alive with flavor." To achieve this, Ash works with Chef Jeff Madura, a graduate of the California Culinary Academy and an up-and-coming chef in his own right. ◆ Located next to the Vintners Inn, John Ash & Co. combines Sonoma charm, vineyard views and terrace dining.

AVERAGE DINNER FOR TWO: $60
DOES NOT INCLUDE WINE, TAX AND GRATUITY

MUSTARDS GRILL

◆

7399 ST. HELENA HIGHWAY 29
YOUNTVILLE, CA 94599
(707) 944-2424

MasterCard & Visa Only
Open Daily • Lunch & Dinner

Proprietors
BILL HIGGINS
BILL UPSON

Chef/Proprietor
CINDY PAWLCYN

Menu Highlights

Appetizers
WARM GOAT CHEESE
WITH BASIL &
PEPPERCORNS •
PASILLA PEPPER WITH
TAMALE STUFFING &
GOLD TOMATO SALSA

Entrées
SONOMA RABBIT WITH
ROASTED PEPPERS &
ROSEMARY
VINAIGRETTE •
YUCATAN-STYLE
CHICKEN BREAST
WITH CHILE &
CHOCOLATE SAUCE

PARTNERS BILL HIGGINS, BILL UPSON AND CINDY PAWLCYN, realizing the restaurant kitchen is the new theatre in American life, placed an open cooking area with an oak, madrone and manzanita wood-burning grill and a birch-burning oven in the middle of their lively Napa Valley restaurant. ◆ Center stage here is Chef Pawlcyn, who follows a self-directed path. A graduate of the University of Wisconsin Restaurant School who trained at the Pump Room in Chicago, Pawlcyn is the brilliant, celebrated menu creator and co-owner of five successful restaurants. Her dishes are stylish and light, characterized by unusual herbs, fish grilled over various types of wood, oven-smoked meats and the North Coast's unusual boutique vegetables. ◆ The ambiance at Mustards is lively and youthful. Local winemakers often gather at the bar to sip one of the many Napa Valley varietals available by the glass.

AVERAGE DINNER FOR TWO: $40
DOES NOT INCLUDE WINE, TAX AND GRATUITY

PIATTI

◆

6480 WASHINGTON STREET
YOUNTVILLE, CA 94599
(707) 944-2070

MasterCard & Visa Only
Open Daily • Lunch & Dinner

Proprietor
GIOVANNI SCALA

Chef/Proprietor
DONNA SCALA

Menu Highlights

Appetizers
PIZZA LA MARGHERITA •
LA BRUSCHETTA: GRILLED
PIATTI BREAD WITH
TOMATOES, GARLIC, BASIL
& OLIVE OIL • SAUTÉED
FRESH SWEETBREADS WITH
ASSORTED MUSHROOMS

Entrées
ROASTED MARINATED
FREE-RANGE CHICKEN
WITH ROASTED POTATOES
• WIDE FETTUCCINI PASTA
WITH SHRIMP, ARUGULA &
FRESH TOMATOES • BEEF
SCALLOPPINE WITH
TOMATO, GARLIC &
OREGANO, SERVED
WITH RIGATONI

GIOVANNI SCALA WAS BORN IN NAPLES, ITALY, BUT IT IS HIS wife, Donna, who cooks like a native. "Even my mother couldn't believe how Italian her cooking is," says Giovanni. And who would believe that in a little more than three years, this young, outgoing couple would, with partners Claude Rouas and Robert Harmon, establish five successful Piattis in California, including one in nearby Sonoma. All are centered on the vibrant cuisine of the charming, self-taught American *Food & Wine* magazine named best up-and-coming chef of 1989. ◆ "Be simple but good" is the Scalas' motto, and it shows in every dish, from the roasted chicken to the pizza and focaccia baked in a wood-burning oven. "Make people feel special" could be their second motto — they will gladly prepare anything their customers ask for if the ingredients are on hand. ◆ With white walls brightened by whimsical murals of vegetables and Italian plates ("piatti"), terracotta tiles on the floors and counters, and a rustic open kitchen, Piatti is perfect for relaxed meals in the company of friends.

AVERAGE DINNER FOR TWO: $45
DOES NOT INCLUDE WINE, TAX AND GRATUITY

THE STARMONT

◆

MEADOWOOD RESORT
900 MEADOWOOD LANE
ST. HELENA, CA 94574
(707) 963-3646

Major Credit Cards
Open Daily for Dinner • Sunday Brunch

Managing Director
MAURICE NAYROLLES

Chef
HENRI DELCROS

Menu Highlights

Appetizers
WARM LOBSTER SALAD •
SCALLOP OF SALMON ON
CRISPY POTATOES

Entrées
STEAMED EMINCE OF
SALMON WITH
VEGETABLES & BASIL
OLIVE OIL SAUCE •
SAUTÉED SEA SCALLOPS
WITH SHALLOT RINGS
& SOY SAUCE •
ROASTED MUSCOVY
BREAST OF DUCK &
POACHED PEARS WITH
BLUEBERRY COULIS

NESTLED IN ITS OWN SMALL VALLEY AT THE END OF A COUN-
try lane, Meadowood is just off the Silverado Trail, minutes outside
St. Helena. Yet this beautiful resort is so secluded and luxurious that
visitors immediately feel miles away from the rest of the world.
Located on the upper level of the clubhouse, The Starmont's formal
interior and large decks look out onto the immaculate golf course,
croquet lawns and the wooded hills beyond. ◆ Born in the Catalogne
region of France, Chef Henri Delcros has practiced his culinary art for
twenty years, first in his own restaurants in France, then in the United
States at The Bistro Garden in Beverly Hills and Chantilly Restaurant
in New York City. His goal is to make The Starmont one of the finest
places to dine in Napa Valley. ◆ Meadowood's extensive wine list,
including over ninety Cabernets, offers wines from the established
Napa Valley wineries as well as selections from the newcomers.

AVERAGE DINNER FOR TWO: $90
DOES NOT INCLUDE WINE, TAX AND GRATUITY

Meadowood
Napa Valley

A World Apart in the Napa Valley

Fireplace Suites, Fairway Grill,
The Starmont Restaurant,
Tennis, Golf, Croquet, Pool,
Massage, Hiking Trails,
Wine School

Meadowood Resort • 900 Meadowood Lane • St. Helena, CA 94574
TEL (707) 963-3646 FAX (707) 963-3532

PREFERRED HOTELS

RELAIS &
CHATEAUX

The exceptional malt
from the heart of Speyside.

ST. ORRES

36601 HIGHWAY ONE SOUTH
NORTH OF TOWN
GUALALA, CA 95445
(707) 884-3335

Credit Cards Not Accepted
Seasonal Schedule • Dinner Only

Proprietor
CHARLES BLACK

Chef/Proprietor
**ROSEMARY
CAMPIFORMIO**

Menu Highlights

Appetizers
SEA URCHIN
MOUSSE • GOAT
CHEESE WITH
SMOKED WILD
BOAR • FRESH BABY
ABALONE • WARM
GARLIC CUSTARD
WITH WILD
MUSHROOMS

Entrées
VENISON WITH WILD
HUCKLEBERRIES •
SILK-SCREEN LOBSTER
RAVIOLONE •
BOAR HIND WITH
FRESH FIGS

ST. ORRES DATES BACK TO 1820, WHEN THE GEORGE ST. ORRES family settled the area now known as Gualala. Today, the reconstructed St. Orres inn and restaurant, designed by Eric Black, overlooks the magnificent Mendocino coast. ♦ Inspired by Russian architecture, the dining room and lodge are dominated by two onion-shaped domes and were built with hundred-year-old timber. Inside, a country-inn atmosphere prevails: an all-natural-wood bar area with a beautiful rock fireplace greets guests at the entrance, and the wall hangings, woven rugs, pictures and lounge furniture are all the work of local artisans. ♦ Every day, under the direction of Rosemary Campiformio, the kitchen prepares food that reflects a California "North Coast" cuisine. Wild boar, venison, wild mushrooms, sea urchin, mussels, salmon and lamb predominate; the produce is locally grown; the bread is fresh-baked daily; and the herbs come straight from the St. Orres garden.

AVERAGE DINNER FOR TWO: $56
DOES NOT INCLUDE WINE, TAX AND GRATUITY

TERRA

◆

1345 RAILROAD AVENUE
ST. HELENA, CA 94574
(707) 963-8931

MasterCard & Visa Only
Closed Tuesday • Dinner Only

Proprietor
LISSA DOUMANI

Chef/Proprietor
HIROYOSHI SONE

Menu Highlights

Appetizers
BARBECUED EEL WITH
JAPANESE CUCUMBER
SALAD • WONTON OF
DUCK LIVER WITH WILD
MUSHROOM SAUCE

Entrées
GRILLED PORK CHOP
WITH YAM PUREE & SPICY
ONION SALAD • OSSO
BUCCO WITH RISOTTO
MILANESE • FRICASSÉE OF
SWEETBREADS WITH
LENTIL & SHERRY WINE
VINEGAR SAUCE • FRIED
QUAIL WITH CHANTERELLE
MUSHROOMS & WILD
RICE RISOTTO

HIROYOSHI SONE, A GRADUATE OF OSAKA'S TSUJI COOKING School, and Lissa Doumani, whose family owns Stag's Leap Winery, met in Los Angeles at Spago, where Hiro was learning the Spago style and Lissa was second pastry chef. After opening Spago in Tokyo for Wolfgang Puck in 1983, Hiro became head chef at Spago/Los Angeles until he left in 1988. ◆ "Hiro said on national television that his dream was to own a restaurant in the wine country," says Lissa with a laugh, "so we had to come here and do this!" ◆ Her warm good humor and Hiro's free-wheeling cooking style found their niche in St. Helena's historic Hatchery Building. Built in 1884, its fieldstone walls, high ceilings and wood beams share the welcoming simplicity of Terra's owners. "We wanted the kind of place where if you drop your fork, you don't feel bad," explains Lissa, "but where you can hear yourself talk." ◆ One topic of conversation is always the food. Hiro's refined amalgam of French, Italian and Japanese cuisines puts Terra at the top of Napa Valley's exciting restaurants.

AVERAGE DINNER FOR TWO: $60
DOES NOT INCLUDE WINE, TAX AND GRATUITY

TRA VIGNE

◆

1050 CHARTER OAK
AT HIGHWAY 29
ST. HELENA, CA 94574
(707) 963-4444

MasterCard & Visa Only
Open Daily • Lunch & Dinner

Proprietor
KEVIN CRONIN

Chef/Proprietor
MICHAEL CHIARELLO

Menu Highlights

Appetizers
GRILLED MOZZARELLA &
PROSCIUTTO IN ROMAINE,
TOMATO VINAIGRETTE •
GRILLED RADICCHIO WITH
BLACK OLIVE &
ZINFANDEL SAUCE

Entrées
FETTUCCINI WITH
GRILLED ARTICHOKE,
SWEET CORN & CHERVIL •
DOUBLE-CUT LAMB CHOPS
WITH BASIL, FENNEL &
BLACK PEPPER • GRILLED
RABBIT WITH MUSTARD,
SAGE & JUNIPER

THE WILDLY SUCCESSFUL PEOPLE AT REAL RESTAURANTS PUT their Midas touch on yet another popular eatery. Located in a landmark stone building (formerly St. George Restaurant), Tra Vigne is Napa Valley's current favorite, attracting an animated crowd of locals and visitors day and night. ◆ The cuisine is what Michael Chiarello likes to call "American food prepared with the heart, hands and eyes of an Italian." Everything is made on the premises — prosciutto, cheeses, breads, pastas, gelati — from ultra-fresh local ingredients. ◆ The decor packs a striking visual punch. Limn Co.'s talented Michael Guthrie has created a neo-Gothic feel, with gilt and modern accents softened by such rustic touches as ash tables and rush-seated chairs. The vine-covered brick courtyard provides a tranquil alternative to the lively action inside.

AVERAGE DINNER FOR TWO: $50
DOES NOT INCLUDE WINE, TAX AND GRATUITY

TRILOGY

◆

1234 MAIN STREET
AT HUNT
ST. HELENA, CA 94574
(707) 963-5507

Major Credit Cards
Dinner Tues-Sat • Lunch Tues-Fri

Proprietors
TIM MOSHER
DON PARISEAU

Chef/Proprietor
DIANE PARISEAU

Menu Highlights

Appetizers
GRILLED SEA SCALLOPS
WITH BLACK OLIVE &
TOMATO VINAIGRETTE •
FETTUCCINI WITH BASIL,
TOMATO & PINE NUTS

Entrées
ROASTED RACK OF LAMB
WITH WHOLE GRAIN
MUSTARD SAUCE •
STEAMED HALIBUT WITH
FERMENTED BLACK BEANS,
GARLIC, GINGER &
SCALLIONS • SAUTÉED
MEDALLIONS OF VEAL
WITH SHIITAKE
MUSHROOMS & SHERRY

THREE YOUNG PARTNERS ARE RESPONSIBLE FOR A FRIENDLY little restaurant where the local crowd comes to relax. Trilogy has everything they need: a warm, low-key atmosphere, outstanding food that doesn't break the calorie bank, and a wine list so extraordinary it earned an award from *The Wine Spectator* after only two years. ◆ Diane Pariseau is the woman in the kitchen, and her modesty belies her expertise. A culinary arts graduate of Johnson & Wales University in Providence, Rhode Island, she apprenticed in classic French cooking. "There is nothing wrong with tradition," she says. "I lighten the classics and try to offer both simple and complex dishes." ◆ Husband Don acts as maître d', and Tim Mosher takes care of the wine list. To accommodate the impressive selection in such a small space, Mosher makes sure he has one bottle of each vintage on hand — a considerable task, since the stock is stored several miles away.

AVERAGE DINNER FOR TWO: $60
DOES NOT INCLUDE WINE, TAX AND GRATUITY

U P   T H E   G R A N D   S T A I R C A S E.

Definitely not your common swallow.

WILD TURKEY

8 years old, 101 proof, pure Kentucky.

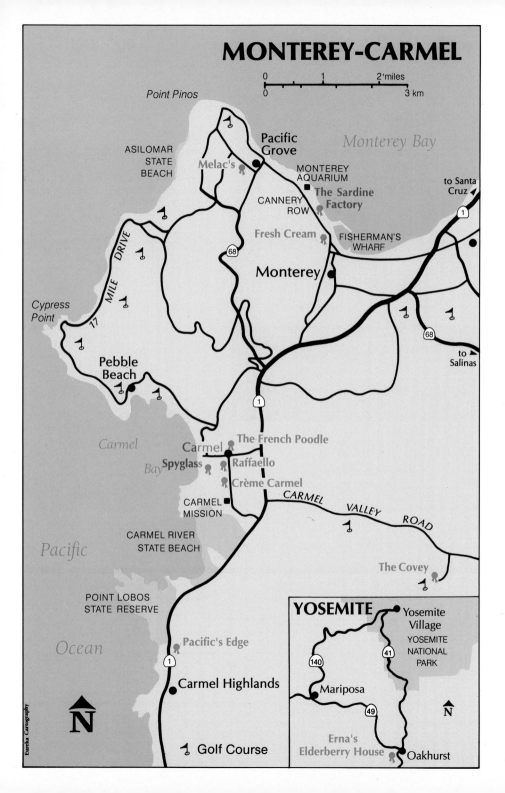

MONTEREY-CARMEL

0   1   2'miles
0   3 km

Point Pinos

Monterey Bay

Pacific
Grove

ASILOMAR
STATE
BEACH

Melac's

MONTEREY
AQUARIUM

The Sardine
Factory

to Santa
Cruz

1

CANNERY
ROW

Fresh Cream

FISHERMAN'S
WHARF

68

Monterey

*Cypress
Point*

68

MILE DRIVE

17

to
Salinas

Pebble
Beach

1

Carmel

The French Poodle

Bay

Carmel

Spyglass

Raffaello

Crème Carmel

CARMEL
MISSION

CARMEL   VALLEY   ROAD

CARMEL RIVER
STATE BEACH

Pacific

POINT LOBOS
STATE RESERVE

The Covey

Ocean

Pacific's Edge

1

Carmel Highlands

YOSEMITE

Yosemite
Village

YOSEMITE
NATIONAL
PARK

140

41

Mariposa

49

Erna's
Elderberry House

Oakhurst

N

⚑ Golf Course

N

Balmy, sunny days, ideal for year-round golf and tennis

QUAIL LODGE
RESORT & GOLF CLUB

uail Lodge is situated on the grounds of a beautiful private country club which, in addition to its 18-hole golf course, provides a wide variety of services for our Quail Lodge guests. The Club dining room offers a tempting and imaginative menu selection for both breakfast and lunch. Our cocktail lounge is perfect for afternoon and evening relaxation.

Please contact Miss Carla Taylor
8205 Valley Greens Drive   Carmel, California 93923
(408) 624-1581

The only Mobil 5-star resort between San Francisco and Los Angeles.

Luxurious guest rooms that change your every expectation into delightful reality

THE COVEY

◆

QUAIL LODGE
8205 VALLEY GREENS DRIVE
CARMEL, CA 93923
(408) 624-1581
Major Credit Cards
Open Daily • Dinner Only

General Manager
CSABA AJAN

Executive Chef
BOB WILLIAMSON

Menu Highlights

Appetizers
BELUGA CAVIAR •
QUENELLES MOUSSELINES:
POACHED MOUSSE OF SEA
SCALLOPS AU GRATIN •
MAINE LOBSTER BISQUE
WITH SHREDDED ARUGULA
& ARMAGNAC CREAM

Entrées
SANTA BARBARA
ABALONE • BREAST OF
PHEASANT STUFFED WITH
SMOKED HAM, DATES &
PINE NUTS • SCAMPI
SINGAPORE, STIR-FRIED
WITH PEA PODS, ASIAN
SPICES, TAMARIND &
COCONUT MILK

EXQUISITE CUISINE WITH A CALIFORNIA FLAIR IN A SPA AND country club atmosphere — it's all yours at Quail Lodge in Carmel, where the undulating Carmel River meanders around a golf course and ten picturesque lakes. ◆ The Covey restaurant's natural wood interiors give it a warm, homey feeling, while its large glass windows and skylights bring in the beauty of the outdoors. ◆ The Covey presents an à la carte menu that reflects Chef Bob Williamson's classical training in Switzerland. His European touch is leavened with a distinctively American style, the result of years spent in Oregon, Chicago and Canada and the availability of California's abundant year-round garden harvests. ◆ Here, sauces are light, the vegetables are al dente and the garnishes feature the artichokes and avocados of the Monterey Peninsula. The wine list features a superb selection of hard-to-find California wines.

AVERAGE DINNER FOR TWO: $70
DOES NOT INCLUDE WINE, TAX AND GRATUITY

CRÈME CARMEL

◆

SAN CARLOS
BETWEEN OCEAN & SEVENTH
CARMEL, CA 93921
(408) 624-0444

MasterCard & Visa Only
Open Daily • Dinner Only

Proprietor
CYNTHIA LING

Chef/Proprietor
CRAIG LING

Menu Highlights

Appetizers
WHITE CORN PANCAKES
WITH MAINE LOBSTER &
LOBSTER SAUCE • FOIE
GRAS SAUTÉED WITH
WHITE WINE &
LATE HARVEST
RIESLING SAUCE

Entrées
KING SALMON WITH
BASIL & TOMATO •
GUINEA FOWL ROASTED
WITH VEGETABLES, HERBS
& FOIE GRAS • ROASTED
LAMB LOIN WITH ROSE-
MARY & GARLIC SERVED
WITH APPLE-
MINT CHUTNEY

SIMPLICITY AND CLARITY ARE CHEF/PROPRIETOR CRAIG Ling's main concerns at Crème Carmel. Clean, straight lines, spare graphics and white linens make up the understated decor. The light, fresh cuisine follows a similar theme. ◆ "Quality is first," says Ling. "We're aware of culinary fashions, but we're suspicious of the avant-garde. Our ideal is to be creative with an underlying directness." ◆ The French character of the menu gains distinction from a subtle lightening of sauces. They do not overwhelm the food; they accent it. ◆ Because Chef Ling likes to take advantage of seasonal products, Crème Carmel's menu offers a printed list of daily specials that is as lengthy as the regular menu. That extends to the desserts, since the wine list includes a singular collection of Sauternes, Barsacs and California Late Harvest dessert wines, often overlooked elsewhere.

AVERAGE DINNER FOR TWO: $65
DOES NOT INCLUDE WINE, TAX AND GRATUITY

THE FRENCH POODLE

◆

JUNIPERO & FIFTH AVENUE
CARMEL, CA 93921
(408) 624-8643

Major Credit Cards
Closed Sunday & Wednesday • Dinner Only

☎ ⅲ

Cellar Master
RICHARD VEDRINES
Proprietor
MICHELE VEDRINES

Chef/Proprietor
MARC VEDRINES

Menu Highlights

Appetizers
DUNGENESS CRAB LEGS
WITH CHAMPAGNE SAUCE,
SEASONED WITH SAFFRON
& CAVIAR • CHICKEN &
DUCK LIVER MOUSSE

Entrées
GRILLED SLICED BREAST
OF DUCK IN OLD PORT
WINE SAUCE • LOIN OF
CALIFORNIA LAMB
SAUTÉED WITH SCALLOPED
POTATOES • FRESH
SALMON WITH MUSCADET
WINE, SHALLOTS &
LEMON BUTTER

AFTER ALMOST THREE DECADES IN CARMEL, THE FRENCH Poodle remains as vital as the day it was opened by Marc and Michèle Vedrines. With Michèle overseeing every detail, from the selection of classical music and individually lit paintings to the elegant remodeling in muted tones of raspberry with black, it has the intimate appeal of a beloved friend. ◆Chef Marc Vedrines has cooked for such famous people as Charles de Gaulle, Gerald Ford and Clint Eastwood, yet he is as modest as his wife is outgoing. A follower of Escoffier who spent eight years as chef at The Lodge in Pebble Beach, Chef Vedrines presents the masterpieces of French cuisine. Authentic and remarkably consistent, his dishes have earned The French Poodle its reputation as the Carmel restaurant French people most love and respect. ◆An excellent wine list leans toward France, and on hand to help diners make the right selection is another talented Vedrines, son Richard. Like his parents, he brings a strong sense of family pride to what has become a Carmel treasure.

AVERAGE DINNER FOR TWO: $60
DOES NOT INCLUDE WINE, TAX AND GRATUITY

FRESH CREAM

◆

100 HERITAGE HARBOR, SUITE F
NEAR FISHERMAN'S WHARF
MONTEREY, CA 93940
(408) 375-9798

MasterCard, Visa & Diners Club Only
Closed Monday • Dinner Only

☎ ⚏

Maître d'	*Chef*
ROSE BRAUN	RICHARD WENZLIK
Proprietor	
KENNETH GARDNER	

Menu Highlights

Appetizers
FRESH LOBSTER RAVIOLI
IN SHRIMP BUTTER •
HOUSEMADE PATÉ OF
FOIE GRAS • RED BELL
PEPPER FLAN WITH
CHICKEN QUENELLES,
APPLE, BLUE CHEESE
& PECANS

Entrées
ROASTED RACK OF LAMB
DIJONNAISE • ROASTED,
BONED DUCKLING WITH
BLACK CURRANTS •
STUFFED MARINATED
SWORDFISH WITH RED
BELL PEPPER BUTTER
& SALSA

JUST BEYOND THE MONTEREY WHARF, YET SEEMINGLY MILES from the crowds, Fresh Cream is a mecca for classical French cuisine prepared with a California flair. Proprietor Ken Gardner commissioned local artist Ami Magill to fill the walls with her California Impressionist paintings, which, together with plentiful fresh flowers and muted tapestried upholstery, create an intimate, charming atmosphere. ◆ An artist in his own right and Fresh Cream's former sous chef, 28-year-old Chef Richard Wenzlik has brought his talents to the forefront at last. Born in Monterey, he began his cooking career at the age of 15, apprenticed in Munich for three years and later graduated from the Culinary Institute of America. ◆ Back in his hometown, he makes the most of its bountiful produce. "I enjoy the challenge of not having a set menu and letting market availability influence my recipes." With Wenzlik running the kitchen, award-winning Fresh Cream is sure to maintain its position as a consistent favorite with local residents and visitors alike.

AVERAGE DINNER FOR TWO: $65
DOES NOT INCLUDE WINE, TAX AND GRATUITY

MELAC'S

◆

663 LIGHTHOUSE AVENUE
PACIFIC GROVE, CA 93950
(408) 375-1743

Major Credit Cards
Dinner Tues-Sat • Lunch Tues-Fri • Sunday Brunch

Proprietor
JACQUES MELAC

Chef/Proprietor
JANET MELAC

Menu Highlights

Appetizers
SMOKED SALMON WITH CREAM, SHALLOTS & OYSTER MUSHROOMS IN PUFF PASTRY • THREE-MUSHROOM RAVIOLI WITH HERB SAUCE & OREGON CHANTERELLES

Entrées
SEA SCALLOPS SEARED IN OLIVE OIL WITH FRESH LEEKS, THYME, LEMON & A TOUCH OF CREAM • BONELESS QUAIL STUFFED WITH SEASONED TABOULI, ROASTED IN WHITE WINE & FRESH THYME

LIKE A WARM COUNTRY RESTAURANT, MELAC'S SACRIFICES glamour for the glory of French cuisine. This cozy restaurant is filled with the dedication and friendliness of its owners, Jacques and Janet Melac. But the husband-wife theme has an interesting twist: American-born Janet is the chef, while French-born Jacques is the man up front. ◆ The two met in Paris where Janet graduated first in her class at the Cordon Bleu School and apprenticed with Gérard Pangaud at the Michelin two-star Boulogne Billancourt. Both worked with Gaston Lenôtre in Paris and later in Texas. Janet cooks every dish to order and changes the menu daily to make use of the freshest seasonal products. Framed by several crisp vegetables, her dishes are generously portioned and attractively presented. ◆ Jacques is a gracious and sensitive host who loves to help patrons pair wine with his wife's creations. He tastes every wine before including it on his list, balancing the best of California's wineries with classic French selections.

AVERAGE DINNER FOR TWO: $50
DOES NOT INCLUDE WINE, TAX AND GRATUITY

PACIFIC'S EDGE

◆

HIGHLANDS INN
HIGHWAY ONE
CARMEL, CA 93921
(408) 624-0471

Major Credit Cards
Open Daily • Lunch & Dinner • Sunday Brunch

Dining Room Manager
TOM FICHERA

Pastry Chef
BRUNO FELDEISEN
Chef
BRIAN WHITMER

Menu Highlights

Appetizers
HOT NEW YORK STATE
FOIE GRAS WITH GLAZED
SHALLOTS • WILD
MUSHROOM RAVIOLI IN
FRESH HERB CONSOMMÉ •
GRILLED QUAIL SALAD
WITH HOT POLENTA
CROUTONS

Entrées
MONTEREY BAY SALMON
WITH FRESH ARTICHOKES
• ROASTED PHEASANT
WITH PARSNIPS &
BLACK OLIVES •
MEDALLIONS OF VEAL
WITH PASTA RISOTTO &
SHIITAKE MUSHROOMS

IN A CLIFFSIDE SETTING ABOVE THE OCEAN, THE GLASS-walled Pacific's Edge restaurant at Highlands Inn features sweeping views of dramatic coast and blue surf framed by towering Monterey pines. ◆ Drawing on the produce of the area — fine local meats, seafood from Monterey Bay, fruits and vegetables from regional specialty farms, even seasonal mushrooms from Big Sur — the Pacific's Edge menu is fresh and creative. In addition to the ever-changing seasonal menu, Chef Brian Whitmer and Pastry Chef Bruno Feldeisen create nightly prix-fixe "Sunset Dinner" menus that are spontaneous and explore the dazzling palette of contemporary cuisine. Complementing the menu, an award-winning wine list features many outstanding wines of California, including those of the Monterey region. ◆ Both modern and historic, Highlands Inn has been a favorite destination for travelers to the spectacular Carmel Highlands coast since 1915.

AVERAGE DINNER FOR TWO: $75
DOES NOT INCLUDE WINE, TAX AND GRATUITY

RAFFAELLO

◆

MISSION STREET
BETWEEN OCEAN & SEVENTH
CARMEL, CA 93921
(408) 624-1541

Major Credit Cards
Closed Tuesday • Dinner-Only

☎ ⦚⦚⦚ ▼

Proprietor
REMO D'AGLIANO

Chef/Proprietor
AMELIA D'AGLIANO

Menu Highlights

Appetizers
MELON & PROSCIUTTO •
SMOKED SALMON •
FETTUCCINI ALLA
ROMANA

Entrées
DUCK WITH BRANDIED
ORANGE SAUCE • FILET OF
SOLE POACHED IN
CHAMPAGNE WITH SHRIMP
• CHICKEN ALLA
FIORENTINA • MONTEREY
BAY PRAWNS WITH BUTTER
& GARLIC • VEAL PICCATA
WITH LEMON SAUCE •
SWEETBREADS WITH
CREAM & WINE SAUCE

IN THE STYLE OF GREAT FLORENTINE ARTISANS AND DECORA-tors, Remo d'Agliano and his wife, Danielle, have created an elegant dining room at Raffaello in picturesque Carmel-by-the-Sea. Beveled glass, etched with the fleur-de-lys of Florence, sets the keynote of the decor. Italian Copedemonte porcelain vases with fresh flowers deco-rate the reception room and each table of the moderately sized dining room. ◆ Proprietor Remo d'Agliano grew up in Florence, where he apprenticed at his family's restaurant. His formal training at the Culinary Academy of Paris broadened his style, adding a pinch of French seasoning to his Italian repertoire. His mother, Amelia d'Agliano, was chef at the family restaurant in Florence, and, at 76, is still in the kitchen today. Mother and son, working in concert, prepare the homemade pasta, wine and cream sauces, scalloppine and a mem-orable *pollo alla Fiorentina*.

AVERAGE DINNER FOR TWO: $50
DOES NOT INCLUDE WINE, TAX AND GRATUITY

SARDINE FACTORY

◆

701 WAVE STREET
ON CANNERY ROW
MONTEREY, CA 93940
(408) 373-3775

Major Credit Cards
Open Daily • Dinner Only

Proprietor
TED BALESTRERI

Proprietor
BERT CUTINO

Menu Highlights

Appetizers

ARTICHOKE CASTROVILLE
FILLED WITH SEASONED
CRABMEAT & CAPERS IN
TOMATO BASIL
HOLLANDAISE

Entrées

FRESH ABALONE IN
THREE STYLES:
MILANESE, DORÉ
& IN GINGER BEURRE
BLANC • TOURNEDOS
CANNERY ROW: PETITE
FILET MIGNON ON
EGGPLANT CANAPÉ WITH
LOBSTER & PRAWNS,
GLAZED IN
MADEIRA SAUCE

ONE OF THE OLDEST RESTAURANTS ON THE MONTEREY Peninsula, the Sardine Factory overlooks historic Cannery Row. The decor reflects the Row's unique past, each of five dining rooms capturing a different mood and sense of elegance. ◆ A fireplace and paintings of sea captains who have sailed into Monterey Bay set the tone for the Captain's Room, while the magnificent Conservatory Room offers fine dining beneath a glass dome surrounded by an enclosed garden. For small gatherings, the Wine Cellar seats up to twenty-six guests who can dine in medieval splendor around a huge, hand-carved refectory table. ◆ The wine and decor here are surpassed only by the bonhomie of proprietors Ted Balestreri and Bert Cutino. They have created an impressive menu, featuring the finest seafood prepared with an Italian flair. To complement the excellent food and special atmosphere, an award-winning wine list offers a superb selection of rare vintages that can be viewed in the wine cellar.

AVERAGE DINNER FOR TWO: $50
DOES NOT INCLUDE WINE, TAX AND GRATUITY

SPYGLASS

◆

LA PLAYA HOTEL
EIGHTH AVENUE & CAMINO REAL
CARMEL, CA 93921
(408) 624-4010
Major Credit Cards
Open Daily • Breakfast, Lunch & Dinner • Sunday Brunch

General Manager
TOM GLIDDEN

Executive Chef
BRYAN CARR

Menu Highlights

Appetizers
SMOKED SALMON WITH
WARM CORN PANCAKES •
SEA SCALLOPS ON
RATATOUILLE WITH FRIED
SPINACH • GOAT CHEESE
& BLACK OLIVE RAVIOLI

Entrées
SEA BASS IN TOMATO
FENNEL FONDUE •
SALMON & ASPARAGUS IN
LOBSTER SAUCE • LAMB
CHOPS WITH ARTICHOKE
SOUFFLÉ IN
ROSEMARY SAUCE

BUILT IN 1904 AS AN ARTIST'S MANSION, THE MISSION-STYLE La Playa Hotel evokes the atmosphere and hospitality of Old Carmel. The elegant Spyglass has a view of the ocean on one side and immaculate flower gardens on the other, with an adjacent terrace perfect for breakfast or lunch on a sunny day. When the fog rolls in, guests seek warmth in a cozy, wood-paneled bar. ◆ Executive Chef Bryan Carr comes to La Playa by way of El Encanto in Santa Barbara. Trained in classic French technique, he worked with such great California chefs as Hubert Keller of Fleur de Lys and Michel Cornu at Auberge du Soleil. Carr, 33, believes in balance and restraint within an innovative style. ◆ "Style is worthless without perspective," he says. "Balancing the components of a sauce, the symmetry of a plate, and the harmony of dishes within the menu is where a chef's influence can be felt."

AVERAGE DINNER FOR TWO: $65
DOES NOT INCLUDE WINE, TAX AND GRATUITY

ERNA'S ELDERBERRY HOUSE

◆

48688 VICTORIA LANE
OFF HIGHWAY 41
OAKHURST, CA 93644
(209) 683-6800

MasterCard & Visa Only
Dinner Wed-Mon • Lunch Wed-Fri • Sunday Brunch

Sommelier
RENEE NICOLE KUBIN

Chef/Proprietor
ERNA KUBIN-CLANIN

Menu Highlights

Sample Menu
GRILLED SHRIMP, SCALLOPS WITH ROE ATTACHED & CRABCAKES WITH CILANTRO-CUCUMBER SAUCE • CREME SÉNÉGALAISE • NECTARINE COMPOTE • ROASTED VEAL MEDALLIONS ON FENNEL, PERNOD SAUCE & PEAR CHUTNEY • NUTTED WILD RICE & SIX SEASONAL VEGETABLES • YOUNG LETTUCES WITH FRUIT VINAIGRETTE • BLACK CURRANT VACHERIN & A CHOCOLATE-MOCHA KISS

"ONE OF THE MOST ELEGANT AND STYLISH RESTAURANTS IN the nation is a little-known place nestled in the foothills of the Sierra Nevada..." With those words in *The New York Times* on July 8, 1987, Craig Claiborne began a paean to Erna's Elderberry House that brought its classic French cuisine to the attention of serious gourmets. Since then, *Gourmet*, *Bon Appetit* and countless other publications have discovered Vienna-born Erna Kubin-Clanin's romantic hideaway just outside of Yosemite. ◆ Built of stone and surrounded by oaks, pines and elderberry bushes, the restaurant has two country-style dining rooms, three private rooms, a natural stone bar and an outdoor terrace. Every detail, from the French fabrics to the antique buffets, is exquisite, chosen by Erna with the same love and care she brings to her six-course, prix-fixe dinners. ◆ Like Craig Claiborne, who came for dinner and stayed three days, guests who wish to prolong the enchantment can look forward to the spring, when Erna's nine-room Château du Sureau will be ready to welcome them.

AVERAGE DINNER FOR TWO: $90
DOES NOT INCLUDE WINE, TAX AND GRATUITY

Have you ever seen a grown man cry?

BUY A FULLY LOADED WINE CELLAR?

Yes. Our wine cellars come fully loaded with every amenity imaginable. You simply add the wine. Select solid oak cabinetry, exquisite French armoire or contemporary glass doors, and more. Our wine cellars recreate the perfect 55°F temperature and 65% humidity of ancient European caves, to protect your valuable wines.

Call for our free catalog of wine cellars, racks, accessories and gifts

800-356-VINO

Monday – Saturday
9:00 a.m. – 5:30 p.m.

Experience the pleasures of owning your own wine cellar.

the WINE ENTHUSIAST

404 Irvington Street • Pleasantville, NY 10570

A GUIDE TO

WORLD CLASS WINES

BY NORMAN ROBY

*A*S THE 1990S UNFOLD, THE QUALITY OF WINE throughout the world has never been higher. Beginning in the 1960s, California upstarts challenged the French and Italian wine industries. Other states and other countries soon followed. After a decade of growth and experimentation in the 1970s, wines of the 1980s took a quantum leap as an international spirit of cooperation began. ♦ Today, winemakers from France, Italy and the United States regularly visit each other's cellars to exchange information and to collaborate on research projects. Without compromising the integrity of their own distinctive wine regions, they have created new approaches to grape growing and winemaking. The result: better wines and more choices than ever before.

WINE TALK

PART OF THE ENJOYMENT OF WINES comes from the conversations they inspire. Quite often the subject is the wine itself. Talking about wine should be easy and relaxed. To help matters along, we have defined the most commonly used words and phrases, with particular emphasis on wine aromas. Most wine commentary proceeds by analogies and suggestions, so trust your instincts, offer your impressions and create descriptions.

♦ **AROMA** All-purpose word for the smell of a wine, which may vary in type (fruity, floral, spicy) and in strength. Aroma is used in the general sense and is usually positive.

♦ **ASTRINGENT** The sensation of a wine that leaves a puckery feel in the mouth and seems to dry out the palate. Most young Cabernets and Zinfandels are astringent. Tannins, from the grapes and oak barrels, contribute to astringency, which is more common in red wines.

+ **AUSTERE** Characteristic of wines that are lean in body and high in acidity but overall on the pleasant side. Usually white wines are likely to be austere in style.

+ **BALANCED** When all of a wine's components (fruit, alcohol, acidity, tannin, oak, sweetness) exist in a harmonious way, the wine is said to be balanced.

+ **BERRY-LIKE** Common aroma description for wines with a fairly distinct fruit character. Zinfandels are often similar to blackberries, Cabernets to black currants and Pinot Noirs to cherries.

+ **BODY** The relative weight of a wine or its viscosity. Ranges from thin to light, to medium, to full-bodied. How a wine clings to the sides of a glass when you swirl it is an indication of its body.

+ **BOUQUET** The odors developed through the aging process as distinguished from the fruity/spicy aroma of the grape.

+ **COMPLEX** Describes both aromas and flavors, and the existence of several facets simultaneously. Multi-dimensional wines are complex. The opposite style is simple or one-dimensional.

+ **CRISP** Wines that are lively on the palate and leave you with a lip-smacking impression similar to tart. Usually results from relatively high acidity.

+ **DRY** Basically, the opposite of sweet.

+ **EARTHY** Exists in varying degrees, from a subtle aroma of dusty weediness to a pungent aroma of mushrooms and truffles. More commonly found in red wines.

+ **FLORAL** Aromas similar to flowers in bloom are said to be floral. White wines such as Johannisberg Riesling and Gewurztraminer are often floral with hints of jasmine and orange blossom. The aroma of violets and roses exists in some Pinot Noirs.

+ **GRASSY** A fresh, lively aroma reminiscent of freshly cut grass, usually considered pleasant, and characteristic of many Sauvignon Blancs. Some Chardonnays and a few Chenin Blancs can be grassy.

+ **HERBACEOUS/HERBAL** Collective terms for aromas hinting of dried herbs such as sage, dill and mint. Herbaceousness is most often found in Sauvignon Blanc.

+ **HONEY** An enticing sweet smell present in some white wines. It is usually a result of *Botrytis cinerea*, "the noble rot."

+ **NOSE** The combination of all odors, aroma, bouquet, oak, etc., detected by the olfactory sense.

+ **OAKED** The aroma derived directly from oak barrel aging and usually described as vanilla-like. The oak is fired to conform to the barrel shape.

+ **SMOKY** An aroma derived mostly from fired oak barrels and often perceived as toasty or roasted, similar to the smell of burning leaves.

+ **SPICY** Many fine wines are characteristically spicy, suggesting cloves, cinnamon and pepper. Zinfandel and Syrah wines tend to be peppery; among white wines, Gewurztraminer can be very spicy.

+ **SUPPLE** A wine that is extremely subtle in a soft, smooth style without being heavy in body.

+ **VEGETATIVE** This covers a range of aromas, from the quite attractive smell of green olives and bell peppers often common to Cabernet Sauvignon and Sauvignon Blanc, to the less attractive green bean and asparagus smells sometimes detected in both types of wine.

+ **YEASTY** The aroma similar to that of fresh-baked bread, which is highly desirable in Champagne and sparkling wines. Some white wines, notably Chardonnay and Sauvignon Blanc, are aged in contact with yeast and acquire subtle yeastiness.

As professional wine tasters in France, we had the pleasure of evaluating over 2,000 California wines.

Now owners of Chateau Potelle in Napa Valley, we are proud to be making California wines with a French accent ... elegant wines that respect the unique personality nature has given these grapes.

Bon Appétit!

Jean-Noel and Marketta Fourmeaux du Sartel

CHATEAU POTELLE
NAPA VALLEY

The California Wines with a French Accent

RENAISSANCE
Estate Bottled Wines from the Sierra Nevada Mountains.
Exclusively.

CALIFORNIA WINES

*C*ALIFORNIA WINES HAVE DEFINITELY COME OF AGE. The finest are now being collected, coveted and cellared with the zeal once reserved for prestigious European wines. Perhaps even more telling is the way the trendsetting restaurants of today, which once may have offered nothing but French wines, proudly offer an array of California wines. ♦ European wine producers have bestowed the ultimate compliment on California as a prime wine region by choosing to become a part of the excitement. Companies such as Möet et Chandon, Piper, Pommery, Roederer, Mouton-Rothschild, Taittinger, G.H. Mumm, Freixenet and many others have joined the dynamic California wine world. ♦ With more than 700 wineries in existence and others on the way, no winery will be able to rest on its laurels. As good as California wines are today, the overall quality level will only continue to rise.

VITICULTURAL AREAS

OF INTEREST TO MOST WINE CONSUMERS is where the grapes were grown — in other words, the wine's origin. By January of 1983 the Treasury Department's Bureau of Alcohol, Tobacco and Firearms tightened the regulations governing place names. The growing region must be defined in terms of boundaries approved by the BATF. Now, when a name like Alexander Valley is used, at least 85 percent of the wine comes from that growing region. However, the winery itself does not have to be located within that region. When the name of a county appears, at least 75 percent of the wine must originate in that county.

♦ **CALIFORNIA** Still commonly used by both small and large producers, this designation means 100 percent of the wine came from California.

♦ **NAPA VALLEY** Running thirty miles in length, this famous wine region keeps on getting bigger and better. Today, with close to 35,000 acres and about 200 wineries, Napa Valley is the leader in wine quality and innovation.

♦ **RUTHERFORD BENCH** Called benchlands, the naturally terraced, iron-rich slopes between Oakville and Rutherford comprise the heart of Cabernet country.

♦ **LOS CARNEROS DISTRICT** One of the most visible viticultural areas, the Los Carneros District falls within both Napa and Sonoma counties. Close to San Francisco Bay, it is a cool growing area producing exquisite grapes. The region is becoming well known for its Pinot Noir and Chardonnay.

♦ **RUSSIAN RIVER VALLEY** This viticultural area follows the course of the Russian River and thus varies widely in its climate. The lower sector is a cool area preferred for its Chardonnay, Pinot Noir and sparkling wine varieties.

♦ **ALEXANDER VALLEY** Located in the inland northeast corner of Sonoma County, the Alexander Valley is large (12,000 acres) and relatively warm. It is quite versatile and reputed for rich Chardonnays and sought-after Cabernet Sauvignons.

♦ **SONOMA VALLEY** Still known as the Valley of the Moon, this historic 5,000-acre region falls on the southwestern side of the Mayacamas mountain range, which separates it from the Napa Valley.

♦ **NORTH COAST** This covers a wide range of vineyards in such diverse counties as Napa, Sonoma, Mendocino, Lake, Marin and Solano.

♦ **CENTRAL COAST** A large viticultural area, the Central Coast includes vineyards in the counties of Monterey, Santa Barbara, San Luis Obispo and San Benito.

♦ **SIERRA FOOTHILLS** Another multi-county place name, Sierra Foothills includes the historic Gold Rush regions of El Dorado, Amador, Yuba and Calaveras counties.

♦ **TEMECULA** Located between San Diego and Riverside County, this viticultural area is tempered by cool breezes and seems to excel in white varietals.

TONIGHT.

⊰ ANOTHER EXCELLENT REASON TO CELEBRATE WITH MUMM CUVÉE NAPA. ⊱

SPARKLING WINES

BY THE LATE 1980S, CALIFORNIA sparkling wines earned international acceptance. Much of the credit for this goes to the influence of the French contingent: Möet et Chandon, Piper-Heidsieck, Mumm, Roederer and Pommery. But the pioneering efforts of hometown favorites such as Schramsberg, Korbel and Iron Horse should not go unnoticed. ♦ The finest sparkling wine producers use the traditional *méthode champenoise*, but do not try to imitate French Champagne. Instead, they produce California sparkling wine with a distinct personality and an exciting fruit accent.

♦ **MUMM NAPA VALLEY:** From its ever-popular Napa Brut Prestige to its ultra-premium Vintage Reserve and special "Winery Lake Cuvée," this producer, formerly Domaine Mumm, enters the 1990s on a hot streak.

♦ **IRON HORSE VINEYARDS:** Owners Barry and Audrey Sterling selected the cool Green Valley area for sparkling wines. Both the Brut and Blanc de Blancs are rich, crisp, perfectly rendered versions.

♦ **DOMAINE CHANDON:** Since the 1970s, Chandon has paved the way with its Brut and Blanc de Noirs. Now its complex, toasty Reserve ranks among the best ever. Chandon also owns the popular Shadow Creek line.

♦ **PIPER-SONOMA:** Its Brut is ideal as an aperitif. Both the Blanc de Noirs and Tête de Cuvée have a little more depth and are meant to be savored. This was one of the most dynamic brands in the 1980s.

♦ **ROEDERER ESTATE:** This handsome Anderson Valley newcomer makes only one sparkler, a Brut as refined and lovely as any. Mature oak-aged wine is added for extra interest.

♦ **SCHARFFENBERGER CELLARS:** This Anderson Valley producer joined forces with Pommery Champagne in 1989. Scharffenberger's Brut and Blanc de Blancs are crisp and lovely.

♦ **SCHRAMSBERG VINEYARDS:** Pioneers Jamie and Jack Davies toiled for years, for good cause. Their Cuvée de Pinot is a sensational, serious Rosé; the toasty Blanc de Blancs, a rare treat.

♦ **GLORIA FERRER:** Located in the Carneros, Gloria Ferrer is owned by Freixenet of Spain. Since 1982 it has found its niche and achieved a distinctive style. The Royal Cuvée has more depth than the charming Brut.

♦ **CULBERTSON WINERY:** Working hard in the Temecula region, Culbertson quickly joined the ranks of quality producers. Its subtle, tasty Brut leads the way and its Cuvée de Frontignan is delicious with dessert.

♦ **DOMAINE CARNEROS:** This exciting and sophisticated first effort from Taittinger's Carneros outpost is remarkably rich and bold in Brut style.

SAUVIGNON BLANC & FUMÉ BLANC

SAUVIGNON BLANC IS ON THE VERGE of becoming California's best all-around white wine. The grape adapts to a wide range of soils and climates, preferring slightly warm to cool temperatures. Winemakers love to experiment with different styles of Sauvignon Blanc by altering the oak-aging routine or by using Semillon as a body-builder. The end result is a wonderful diversity.

- **CAKEBREAD CELLARS:** The Cakebread family has worked long and hard to convince the world that Sauvignon Blanc is a first-class wine. By the end of the 1980s, theirs had become a model of beauty and complexity.

- **MATANZAS CREEK WINERY:** For years, this winery has turned out focused, beautifully crafted Sauvignon Blancs that age well, yet are also delicious upon release. They are unusually rich on the palate.

- **SILVERADO VINEYARDS:** Restrained in varietal grassiness, this wine is otherwise a treasure chest of ripe, juicy, fruity flavors.

- **KENWOOD VINEYARDS:** In the winner's circle every year since 1983, Kenwood favors an intense grassy/weedy style that is magically controlled to produce round, smooth flavors.

- **HUSCH VINEYARDS:** From inland Mendocino, Husch partly barrel-ferments its version to capture oak subtlety, attractive varietal fruit and crisp acidity.

- **DRY CREEK VINEYARD:** Owner David Stare practically defined the fresh-cut grass, medium-bodied, focused style of Fumé Blanc from Sonoma County. Recent vintages contain a subtle oak component.

- **WILLIAM WHEELER WINERY:** Blending wines from several Sonoma County appellations, winemaker Julia Iantosca has been quietly succeeding with wines of subtlety, richness and unusually brisk acidity.

- **HANNA WINERY:** A pretty wine from an unusual label, Hanna's Sauvignon Blanc is herbal in aroma and smooth in texture. Aged for several months in new French oak, it is luscious on the palate.

- **SIMI WINERY:** Under Zelma Long's guidance, Simi's Sauvignon Blanc is subtle and stylish, with depth and a lingering finish.

- **McDOWELL VALLEY VINEYARDS:** From inland Mendocino, the Keehn family struck gold with its racy yet smooth Fumé Blanc.

- **ROBERT PEPI WINERY:** Both Robert Pepi and son Robert, Jr., prefer Sauvignon Blanc wines to all others. Since 1981, their versions have offered excellent flavors and balance with a hint of wood.

CALIFORNIA

CHARDONNAY

CHARDONNAY, THE WORLD'S GREATEST WHITE WINE, has almost become a victim of its own popularity. Just about every winery in and out of California now bottles a Chardonnay — with predictably uneven results. Whether made in a crisp apple, medium-bodied style, or an oak-enhanced, buttery smooth, tropical fruit style, California's leading Chardonnays are more refined and better balanced today than they were a decade ago.

+ **KISTLER VINEYARDS:** Steve Kistler and winemaker Mark Bixler have recently produced stunning, unbeatable Chardonnays. From their small Sonoma Valley winery, they make an Estate Chardonnay as well as three other beauties: McCrea Vineyard, Dutton Vineyard and Durrell Vineyard.

+ **MATANZAS CREEK WINERY:** Sandra and Bill MacIver's wines have been a marvel of consistency and quality since they opened their winery in the Bennett Valley. They are rich, complex, and superbly balanced.

+ **CUVAISON WINERY:** Once Cuvaison's Carneros vineyards were in full production, winemaker John Thatcher launched a series of elegant, silky, soft Chardonnays that are a sheer delight.

+ **CHATEAU MONTELENA:** Year in and year out, Montelena ranks among the top Chardonnays with both its Alexander Valley and Napa Valley bottlings. Winemaker Bo Barrett has an unblemished Chardonnay record.

+ **GRGICH HILLS:** Mike Grgich continues his winning ways with Chardonnay from his own winery. Since 1977, he has put his stamp on wines of great varietal character and harmony.

+ **ROBERT KEENAN:** Of two Chardonnays bottled, Keenan's Napa Valley version captures ripe apple fruitiness and toasty oak.

+ **BURGESS:** Tom Burgess relies on his own "Triere Vineyard" in Yountville for his Chardonnays, produced in the classic winemaking style of White Burgundies. They are beautifully balanced wines with toasty oak flavors.

+ **KENDALL JACKSON WINERY:** Winemaker Jed Steele is famous for an array of impeccable Chardonnays. Among them, the Proprietor's Reserve is loaded with character, and the Vintner's Reserve is sleek and lovely.

+ **FAR NIENTE VINEYARDS:** Recent vintages from this winery are now barrel-aged in a giant underground cave designed for Chardonnay. The winery is noted for its bold, full-blown style.

+ **MORGAN WINERY:** Owner-winemaker Dan Lee knows every vineyard in Monterey and selects from the best to produce well-knit, well-focused Chardonnays, which are now receiving their due.

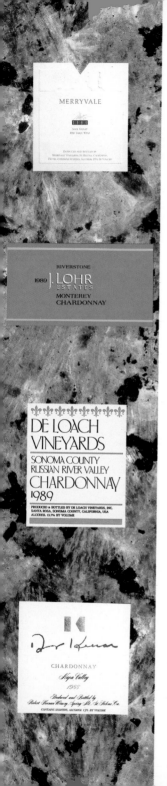

◆ **DE LOACH VINEYARDS:** From Sonoma's Russian River region, De Loach Chardonnays best typify the forward, juicy appeal of the grape.

◆ **FLORA SPRINGS:** This family-owned winery has some of the finest vineyards in the Napa Valley, and uses only a portion to make its lovely, balanced barrel-fermented Chardonnay.

◆ **CLOS DU BOIS:** A winery with several fine Chardonnays, Clos du Bois makes one from the Calcaire Vineyard that is often mistaken for a great French wine.

◆ **EDNA VALLEY VINEYARDS:** In most vintages, this winery produces wines that are big and full, yet display all the charms of Chardonnay.

◆ **RAYMOND VINEYARD:** Among the best-known, most respected wine families in Napa Valley, the Raymonds make balanced, poised Chardonnays. The Reserve offers an extra helping of ripeness and oak.

◆ **J. LOHR ESTATE:** Located in San Jose, Lohr owns vineyards in Monterey. Its flagship is the Riverstone Vineyard, which is used for sleek, spicy and lemony crisp Chardonnay.

◆ **WILLIAM HILL:** From his own vineyards, Hill makes a barrel-fermented special Chardonnay combining ripe fruit and rich oak tones in a style that can be aged and is hard to surpass for harmony.

◆ **FERRARI CARANO WINERY:** One of Sonoma County's latest success stories, this winery combines the apple and tropical fruit notes typical of Alexander Valley grapes with subtle oak flavors. The result is lovely.

◆ **SIMI WINERY:** Using grapes from Sonoma and Mendocino, Simi keeps pace with the fast pack. Its silky-smooth, well-knit regular Chardonnay improves each year, and its Reserve is as rich as Chardonnay can be.

◆ **HANNA VINEYARD:** Dr. Hanna, a heart surgeon, has acquired and developed some of the best vineyards in Sonoma. His winery's barrel-fermented Chardonnay offers ripe apple aromas and a touch of oak.

◆ **MERRYVALE VINEYARDS:** Specializing in two wines, Merryvale buys grapes from the most famous growers in Napa Valley. The Chardonnay, aged in new French oak, has been outstanding in recent vintages.

◆ **FRANCISCAN VINEYARD:** From its Oakville Estate in Napa, this winery is emerging as a class act. The well-ripened fruit flavors and buttery style of its Chardonnays are easy to enjoy.

◆ **TREFETHEN VINEYARDS:** Since 1977, the Trefethens have created a unique style of Chardonnay that is subtle yet age-worthy. The wine merges ripe apple aromas with light oak spice.

◆ **ST. CLEMENT VINEYARDS:** Vintner Dennis Johns creates focused, varietal Chardonnays from grapes grown primarily in the winery's estate vineyard in the Carneros region of Napa Valley. They have excellent aging potential.

Our winemaker's palette.

Rest assured we know the proper spelling of *palate*. But our winemaker is also blessed with a rich and intricate *palette*.

Winery Lake — one of 14 Sterling Vineyards in the Napa Valley.

It is the Napa Valley. Here, 14 vineyards of exceptional quality provide a brilliant spectrum of grape varieties and styles with which to create. Each possesses a unique set of microclimates and soil conditions. And each is farmed and harvested under the attentive care of Sterling Vineyards. It is this "palette" that makes possible the exquisite balance, complexity, and character which distinguish the wines of Sterling Vineyards.

To fully appreciate Sterling character, we invite you to experience the products of our winemaker's palette: our selection of Sterling estate-bottled varietals, vineyard-designated bottlings, and Sterling Reserve. We think you'll agree that here, indeed, is art. For the palate.

The Wines of Sterling Vineyards.

PINOT NOIR

A WINE LOVER'S WINE, PINOT NOIR is possibly an acquired taste. But since it is demanding to grow and insists on cool locations, fine Pinot Noir will never be available in enormous quantities. So far the best Pinot Noir comes from four cool locales — the Carneros District, Sonoma's Russian River Valley, Mendocino's Anderson Valley and Santa Barbara County. At its finest, Pinot Noir is light in color, full in body, velvety in texture, and reminiscent of smoky cherries — sometimes with a hint of beef, bacon and mushrooms. It sounds like a strange mix, but Pinot Noir is a wine of contrasts.

- **ACACIA WINERY:** Now part of the Chalone family, Acacia continues its champion ways with multiple bottlings. For true cherry-like character and velvety texture, the St. Clair bottling is tops.
- **DEHLINGER WINERY:** Winemaker Tom Dehlinger, a perfectionist among perfectionists, is making waves with a rich style of Pinot Noir that emphasizes cherries and spices.
- **CARNEROS CREEK WINERY:** Much of the credit for improved Pinot Noir in California should go to Francis Mahoney, whose experimental vineyard has proven invaluable. His own bottlings from the Carneros are among the richest and ripest, yet also among the most supple.
- **CALERA:** Now with four small vineyards at his disposal, Josh Jensen has added to his bottlings of intense, concentrated and long-lived Pinots. The perennial favorites are the Selleck and Jensen Pinots, each highly distinct.
- **ZACA MESA:** One of the pioneers in Santa Barbara, Zaca Mesa is back on track with its Reserve Pinot Noirs. The latest vintages combine cherries with spicy, smoky oak tones for a complex, mouth-filling wine.
- **SAINTSBURY:** Dick Ward and David Graves capture the sleek, satiny, pure cherry character from the Carneros region. Year after year, theirs is one of the best balanced Pinots.
- **WILD HORSE WINERY:** Ken Volk's winery is in Templeton, but he selects from the finest growers in Santa Barbara to offer a rich style of Pinot Noir that reminds many experts of a fine Côte de Nuits.
- **BUENA VISTA:** One of the oldest names in California, Buena Vista has an extraordinary 350-acre vineyard in the Carneros. From it, Jill Davis makes a delicate but varietally correct Pinot Noir, with charm, subtlety and just the right degree of toasty oak.
- **STERLING VINEYARDS:** From the legendary Winery Lake Vineyard, Sterling's rendition opts for subtle cherry fruit, enriching oak and overall elegance.

Carneros Chardonnay

Beaulieu Vineyard

**THE PRIVATE
COLLECTOR'S
PRIVATE
RESERVE™**

To Send a Gift of Beaulieu Vineyard, Call 1-800-272-5883

Beaulieu Vineyard, Rutherford, Napa Valley, California · USA

MERLOT

THE GRAPE OF THE FABLED POMEROL, Merlot attracted belated interest from growers and winemakers in the late 1960s. Since then, Merlot has dramatically increased in stature among consumers and in importance among collectors. At its best, Merlot offers depth along with a mouth-filling, mouth-coating texture, and an aroma of herbs, spices, cherries and black currants.

♦ **DUCKHORN VINEYARD:** The pacesetter for Merlot since 1978, wine-maker Tom Rinaldi calls Duckhorn's Three Palms the most intense, Vine Hill the next in line, and Napa Valley the first to enjoy.

♦ **MATANZAS CREEK VINEYARD:** From Sonoma County, this Merlot rises above the rest because of its incredible richness and finesse. With an aroma of spices and herbs, it has enough tannin to age long and well.

♦ **MARKHAM VINEYARDS:** One of the best-kept secrets of the 1980s, Markham's Merlots are beautifully balanced, with just the right degree of sweet oak, soft tannin and varietal intensity.

♦ **CUVAISON WINERY:** Emerging as a class winery in the 1980s, Cuvaison achieved tremendous success with Merlot. Aromas of cedar and fruit combine with ripeness and smooth oak in this voluptuous rendition.

♦ **FRANCISCAN VINEYARDS:** Franciscan has offered velvety smooth Merlots with plenty of spicy, jammy varietal fruit since the early 1980s. Excellent depth assures good cellaring potential.

♦ **STERLING VINEYARDS:** Among the first producers of Merlot, Sterling now favors finesse and elegance in style. The aroma typically combines berries and herbaceousness in a distinctive, medium-intense version.

♦ **ROBERT KEENAN:** Located along Spring Mountain in Napa Valley, Keenan is noted for wines of great intensity. Blended with Cabernet Franc, its ripe, powerful Merlots are no exception.

♦ **GUNDLACH BUNDSCHU:** From their Rhinefarm Vineyard, the Bundschus make one of the few genuine, full-bodied, ripe-styled Merlots.

♦ **LOUIS M. MARTINI:** In the late 1960s, this winery was the first to bottle a Merlot. Martini is on the upsurge lately, with Merlot leading the way.

♦ **NEWTON VINEYARDS:** From terraced mountain vineyards, Newton makes fragrant, fleshy Merlots. Cabernet Franc is added for a style similar to Bordeaux's Pomerol.

♦ **GUENOC WINERY:** One of the wineries to watch in the 1990s, Guenoc produces forthright, supple Merlots.

♦ **VICHON WINERY:** Owned by Robert Mondavi's three children, Vichon is making rich, complex Merlot on the same high level as all Mondavi-influenced reds.

A Family Tradition of Winemaking Excellence

Burgess Cellars • St. Helena, CA 94574 • (707) 963-4766 • TOURS BY APPOINTMENT

CABERNET SAUVIGNON

WITHOUT QUESTION, CABERNET SAUVIGNON has been California's greatest wine for thirty years or longer. Now, with more producers and furious competition, the overall quality is better than ever. Winemakers have become more skilled at their trade, using blenders such as Cabernet Franc and/or Merlot when they feel a more exciting wine will result. At the same time, experienced wine-makers who began in the 1970s are applying their accumulated experience and wisdom to produce more subtle, elegant and restrained Cabernets. All three factors come into play in the best vintages of the 1980s — '85, '86 and '87.

✦ **CAYMUS VINEYARDS:** Winemaker Chuck Wagner has the Midas touch with Cabernet. The rare Special Selection is superb and long-lived, but the Estate Bottled is always outstanding. Even the Napa Cuvée is special.

✦ **SILVER OAK CELLARS:** A Cabernet specialist, Silver Oak ages its wines in cask and bottle until they are fully developed and smooth. As a result, the Alexander Valley bottling and the Napa Valley version are so beautiful they should be on every fine wine list.

✦ **BEAULIEU VINEYARD:** One of the benchmarks of Napa Valley Cabernet, the winery's Private Reserve continues to rank high on every collector's list. Ripe, earthy and tannic, it ages well.

✦ **JORDAN VINEYARDS:** From its large Alexander Valley plantings, Jordan produces a charming, smooth-as-silk Cabernet Sauvignon. Winemaker Rob Davis blends in Merlot for extra roundness and complexity.

✦ **ROBERT MONDAVI WINERY:** Both the regular bottling and the Reserve improve a little each year and remain among the best of their price category. Held for three years in new French oak, the recent Reserves have exceeded all expectations.

✦ **BERINGER VINEYARDS:** This venerable Napa Valley name has been making truly distinctive, top-notch Reserve Cabernets since the late 1970s. Selecting from the finest Napa grapes, Beringer's winemaster, Ed Sbragia, has been on a roll since 1984.

✦ **DUNN VINEYARDS:** Randy Dunn (formerly of Caymus) founded a small winery on Howell Mountain in 1979. Every vintage since then has been coveted by collectors. Both the Howell Mountain and Napa Valley Cabernets are fabulous.

✦ **CLOS DU VAL:** Located along the Silverado Trail, Clos du Val was among the first to show the potential of the Stag's Leap district. Winemaster Bernard Portet's supple Cabernets reveal the French influence.

♦ **FAR NIENTE:** In the magnificently refurbished winery, Far Niente turns out vintages of Cabernet Sauvignon that have become highly sought after. Made from Napa Valley grapes, Far Niente Cabernets are rich, full and well-balanced for aging.

♦ **RAYMOND VINEYARDS:** The Raymonds quietly go about making quality Cabernets, then let the wines do the talking. Their Private Reserves and regular Napa Valley bottlings are textbook perfect.

♦ **STERLING VINEYARDS:** Long a favorite among collectors, Sterling's Reserves are sturdy and slow to reach maturity, but heavenly wines for those who can wait.

♦ **WILLIAM HILL:** Bill Hill uses only low-yielding grapes from his mountainside vineyards. The results are wines of concentration and character, but with enough balance to age gracefully for six to ten years.

♦ **RIDGE VINEYARDS:** Arguably the most distinctive and long-lived of all California Cabernets, Ridge's Monte Bello is packed with black currant, earthy and spicy components, as well as considerable tannin for aging.

♦ **INGLENOOK NAPA VALLEY:** One of the early "great" ones, Inglenook has recaptured its past glories. Now with two Cabernets, the Reserve Cask and Reunion, Inglenook is once again outstanding.

♦ **ST. CLEMENT VINEYARDS:** Well-knit, with perfect balance, the Cabernets from St. Clement are amazingly harmonious and consistently excellent. Their aromas of currants and herbs are the essence of Cabernet.

♦ **SILVERADO VINEYARDS:** Carving out a new style of Cabernet, winemaker Jack Stuart emphasizes fruit and soft tannins in his wines. Though accessible when young, they will reward cellaring.

♦ **JOSEPH PHELPS VINEYARDS:** By 1980, Phelps had made its mark on the Cabernet world. Its vineyard-designated wines — Eisele Vineyard and Backus Vineyard — rank among the finest. But the more plentiful Napa Valley bottling is often one of the most surprising.

♦ **V. SATTUI WINERY:** Known as a great picnic area, the Sattui winery in St. Helena is serious about its Cabernets and has the gold medals to prove it. The Preston Vineyard has a focused, ripe fruit style.

♦ **LYETH WINERY:** Founded in 1981, Lyeth produces Cabernets that are concentrated and attractive in their youth.

♦ **BURGESS CELLARS:** The Vintage Selection Cabernets from Burgess are so consistently fine that they deserve even more praise than they receive. From old mountain vineyards in Napa, they age well.

♦ **GROTH VINEYARDS:** Since 1985, winemaker Nils Venge has produced some of the hottest Cabernets.

♦ **FETZER VINEYARDS:** Popular for its Barrel Select Cabernets, this admired family winery has a Reserve that is now winning over collectors.

Far Niente

A Napa Valley Wine Estate

Rare
Treasure,
Recently
Unearthed

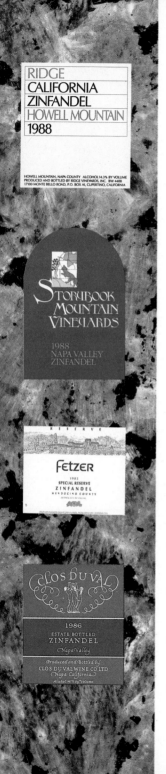

ZINFANDEL

ZINFANDEL HAS BEEN ON A FAST ROLLER-COASTER RIDE since being discovered in the late 1960s. As the '90s unfold, it is again on top as a highly esteemed red dinner wine that is a remarkably versatile food companion. The roster of producers has changed many times, and only those firmly committed to Zinfandel as a serious, sophisticated wine continue to offer it. The appellations emerging as excellent for Zinfandel are Dry Creek Valley, Mendocino, Sonoma Valley, Howell Mountain and other Napa Valley hillside regions.

- **RIDGE VINEYARDS:** For more than twenty vintages, Ridge has shown the way by offering Zinfandels from several appellations. The Geyserville is massive and handsome, the Lytton Springs a close second.
- **STORYBOOK MOUNTAIN:** A Zinfandel specialist located north of Calistoga, Storybook offers a Napa Valley and an Estate Reserve Zinfandel. Both are elegant, balanced wines capable of long aging.
- **FETZER VINEYARDS:** A longtime advocate of Zinfandel from Mendocino County, Fetzer makes a Ricetti Reserve and a Mendocino Reserve. Both display a strawberry, spicy character.
- **CHATEAU SOUVERAIN:** After its major renovation phase, this winery has focused on its wines. Among the best is its Zinfandel from the Dry Creek Valley, a spicy, medium-bodied beauty.
- **QUIVIRA VINEYARDS:** Another winner from Dry Creek, Quivira Zinfandel offers jammy fruit and good depth. It is superbly balanced.
- **BURGESS CELLARS:** Since the early 1970s, Tom Burgess has made Zinfandels from other hillside vineyards in Napa Valley. His wines are very aromatic and berry-like.
- **RAVENSWOOD:** Joel Peterson is a Zinfandel fanatic. He offers a Sonoma County, a Dickerson and a Vintner's Blend, all complex and rich.
- **LYTTON SPRINGS WINERY:** Using vineyards planted in 1900, Lytton Springs produces big, intense, ripe Zinfandels with tremendous flavor concentration. They are the epitome of Sonoma Zinfandel.
- **CLOS DU VAL:** French-born winemaster Bernard Portet works with Zinfandel to capture the berry and spice character of the grape in a refined, medium-bodied French style.
- **FROGS LEAP WINE CELLAR:** For several vintages, this winery has offered Zinfandels that capture the essence of blackberry components in a polished, richly flavored style.
- **KENWOOD VINEYARDS:** Always on target, Kenwood has added a Zinfandel from the Jack London Ranch that competes with its highly successful Sonoma Valley version. Both offer lovely fruit flavors.

MÉRITAGE & PROPRIETARY RED WINES

IN THE 1980S MANY CALIFORNIA WINEMAKERS became intrigued by Bordeaux wines and began trying to replicate those famous clarets. By combining Cabernet Sauvignon with Merlot, Cabernet Franc and — when available — Malbec and Petit Verdot, winemakers created a type of wine unlike any one varietal. Before too long, an entire new category of wine was created from traditional Bordeaux varieties and christened "Méritage."

- ♦ **OPUS ONE:** The result of the partnership between the Robert Mondavi Winery and Château Mouton-Rothschild, Opus One made its debut in 1979. Ever since then, this rich, super-refined wine has been ferreted away by collectors aware of its long-term aging ability.
- ♦ **CAIN FIVE:** As soon as they started their winery in 1981, Joyce and Jerry Cain decided to create this red from the five Bordeaux grapes. Since its 1985 inaugural wine, Cain Five has been highly acclaimed.
- ♦ **INSIGNIA:** First made in 1974, Insignia from Joseph Phelps Vineyards was the California pioneer of the type. This style tends to display cedar and currants in the aroma, richness and suppleness in the flavors.
- ♦ **MARLSTONE:** Entered by Clos du Bois, Marlstone has ranked among the best for elegance and sheer beauty since it was introduced in 1981.
- ♦ **MERRYVALE:** Using grapes from pedigreed Napa Valley Vineyards, the owners of Merryvale, who also own the Sunny St. Helena Winery, produce only Chardonnay and this rich, long-lived red, blended from Cabernet Sauvignon, Merlot and Cabernet Franc.
- ♦ **TRILOGY:** Made from three grapes — Cabernet Sauvignon, Merlot and Cabernet Franc — Trilogy is the pride of Flora Springs. Its owners select grapes from their estate vineyards in Rutherford to produce this compact, limited-volume, well-knit Méritage blend.
- ♦ **REUNION:** Made from three famous vineyards in Napa Valley, Reunion is a rich, well-wrought wine that shows how long and well the best California wines can age.
- ♦ **THE POET:** Created by Cosentino Winery in Napa, The Poet is one of the most fragrant of all Méritage blends. Winemaker Mitch Cosentino imparts an extra touch of oak spice to balance the wine's ripeness.
- ♦ **OAKVILLE ESTATE MÉRITAGE:** From Franciscan Vineyards, this relative newcomer, a blend of Cabernet Sauvignon and Merlot, is round on the palate, but boasts a powerful scent of fruit, oak and spice.
- ♦ **A TRIBUTE, BENZIGER OF GLEN ELLEN:** This family winery and upscale label are capable of great quality, as demonstrated by their Cabernet-Merlot-Cabernet Franc blend, a tribute to founder Bruno Benziger.

DESSERT WINES

DESSERT-STYLE WINES GENERALLY FALL into two distinct types. The first includes wines labeled Late Harvest or something similar — most often made from Riesling or Semillon and, occasionally, from Sauvignon Blanc. *Botrytis cinerea*, a naturally occurring mold, concentrates the grape sugars and imparts exotic fragrances and flavors. These wines depend on natural conditions and are not produced every year. ◆ The second type of dessert wine, typified by Sherry, Port and Madeira, is fortified by the addition of grape spirits and produced every year.

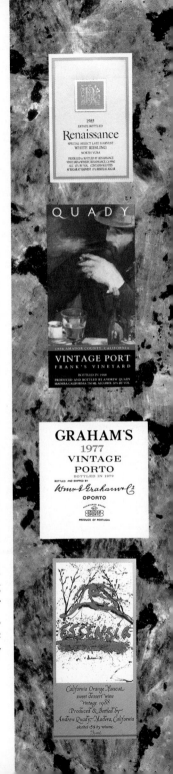

◆ **LATE HARVEST RIESLINGS:** Since the mid-1970s, Château St. Jean and Joseph Phelps have led the way with often stunning Late Harvest and Select Late Harvest Rieslings. Freemark Abbey's rich Edelwein Gold is intensely special. Other standouts are Hogue Cellars and Château Ste. Michelle from Washington State, and Hidden Cellars, Renaissance Vineyards and Navarro from California.

◆ **SAUTERNES:** From the southern Bordeaux district, Sauternes is a wonder of nature made possible by the noble rot. Because of the risks and extra labor involved, Sauternes is the world's most expensive wine to produce. As always, Château d'Yquem is the top name — and it is heaven. Many others are making serious Sauternes, including Château Suduiraut, Rieussec, Climens, Filhot, Sigalas Rabaud and Lafaurie-Peyraguey.

◆ **SPECIAL MUSCAT WINES:** One of the most ancient wines, Muscat de Frontignan is a rare treat, best exemplified today by Beaulieu Vineyard's oak-aged Muscat de Frontignan. Quady Winery makes two tantalizing, lightly fortified wines: a decadent dessert wine named Essencia, and the enchanting Elysium, made from Black Muscat. For decades, one truly special wine named Moscato, a delicate, opulent, frothy wine, has come from Louis M. Martini.

◆ **PORT WINES:** This deep, full-flavored fortified wine is usually enjoyed after a meal. From Portugal come fine Vintage Ports that require cellaring for a minimum of ten years, but preferably twenty. The sought-after brands today are Warre, Fonseca, Cockburn, Sandeman, Croft, Graham's, Dow and Taylor. Those upholding the Port tradition in California are Shenandoah Vineyards, J.W. Morris (try the Vintage Port), and Quady Winery, with its Vintage Port and Port of the Vintage.

Norman Roby *is director of the Academy of Wine in Mendocino and a columnist for* THE WINE SPECTATOR.

TONIGHT, BE FRENCH.

MOUTON-CADE

by Baron Philippe de Rothsch

FRANCE & ITALY

*T*HE FRENCH AND ITALIANS HAVE BEEN MAKING WINE LONGER than anyone else. Although France set the standard in both quality and volume over the centuries, Italy perfected its own unique regional varieties. Today, each country produces nearly two billion gallons a year. ◆ The first lesson in understanding European wines is how they are identified. Unlike California wines, which are labeled by producer and varietal, French and Italian wines stress where the grapes originated — the appellation of origin. Most French and many Italian wines are identified by region, such as Chablis, Bordeaux or Chianti. ◆ The flavors and aromas of the wines mirror their growing region and climate, or their *terroir*, the French term for soil or ground. Since French and Italian wine labels emphasize appellation of origin, the vintner's name may appear only in small print. ◆ Appellation of origin does not promise quality, but it does guarantee authenticity. Because it is so important, the use of place names is strictly controlled by the French and Italian governments. ◆ A second important consideration is vintage, the year the grapes were picked and made into wine. Maintaining the same quality and taste year after year is impossible, particularly since Europeans tend to select difficult sites and climates for their grape plantings. ◆ As a result, the wines produced in a specific area can vary in unexpected ways. In good years, the wines have a more intense, typical flavor. In bad years, the wines are dull, weak and thin. The best years have the highest numbers. A simple rule to remember: keep great vintages for tomorrow, drink lesser vintages today. ▼

VINTAGE CHART

		1960	1961	1962	1963	1964	1965	1966	1967	1968	1969	1970	1971	1972	1973	1974	1975	1976	1977	1978	1979	1980	1981	1982	1983	1984	1985	1986
FRANCE	Bordeaux	5	10+	8	4	7	4	9+	7	5	6	10	8	5	6	5	9	8	6	8+	7	6	7	10	8	6	10+	9
	Red Burgundy	4	9	8	3	7	3	7	5	3	10	7	10	8	6	4	5	9	3	9	8	7	6-	6	8+	5	10+	8-
	White Burgundy	4	8	8	4	8	3	8	7	4	9	7	8	9	7	8	6	8	5	9	8	6	7-	7	8-	6	10	8+
	Rhone Valley	10	9	8	4	8	4	8	7	5	9	8	9	8	7	6	6	9	6	9+	8+	8-	6	9	8+	7+	10	8
ITALY	Chianti	5	7	6	4	9	6	7	8	9	8	9	10	5	6	8	9	6	9	8+	8	7	9	10	8	6	10	8+
	Barolo & Piedmont	5	10	7	6	10	7	4	8	6	7	9	10	N/A	5	8	6	5	6	10	8	7	6	10	8	5	10	8
	Brunello	4	9	5	4	9	4	8	9	8	7	10+	10	4	7	6	10	5	7	8	7	8	8	10	7	5	10	9

10 – *Outstanding*   **9** – *Excellent*   **8**– *Well Above Average*   **7** – *Slightly Above Average*   **6** – *Average*
5 – *Slightly Below Average*   **4** – *Well Below Average*   **1 to 3** – *Total Loss*   **N/A** – *Not produced that year*

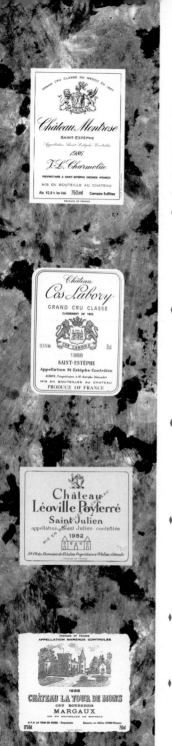

BORDEAUX

EVEN THE CASUAL AMERICAN WINE-LOVER has become an avid collector of red Bordeaux, also known as Claret. To create Bordeaux, the winemaker blends Cabernet Sauvignon, Merlot, Cabernet Franc, Malbec and Petit Verdot grapes into whatever combination will yield the best of the vintage. A 260,000-acre appellation, Bordeaux is divided into many sub-appellations.

✦ **ST. ESTEPHE:** Once synonymous with rough, slow-developing wines, St. Estèphe has been offering redesigned wines since about 1982. Typically ripe, rich and concentrated, they now have a welcome elegance and accessibility. While the established châteaux of Montrose and Cos d'Estournel remain at the top, challengers include Les Ormes de Pez, de Pez, Phelan-Ségur, Calon-Ségur, Cos Labory, Haut-Marbuzet, Le Crock and Meyney.

✦ **PAUILLAC:** Home to three legendary First Growths, Lafite, Latour and Mouton-Rothschild, Pauillac is famous for wines that combine intensity of flavor (cassis, cedar, berries) with finesse and subtlety. These characteristics are worshipped by collectors, envied by fellow wine producers, and duplicated by no one. Other châteaux names to look for include Pichon-Lalande, Pichon-Longueville-Baron, Lynch-Bages, Grand-Puy-Lacoste and Haut Batailley.

✦ **ST. JULIEN:** Refined and subtle, the St. Juliens have just enough concentration to appeal to those who like richness. The finest can age long and well. The stars of the 1980s are Ducru-Beaucaillou, Léoville-Las-Cases and Beychevelle; rapidly rising châteaux include Gloria, Gruaud-Larose, Léoville-Poyferré and Talbot. Ever consistent are Léoville-Barton and Langoa-Barton.

✦ **MARGAUX:** Since the 1980s, the wine with more finesse than all the others comes from the town of Margaux and has been labeled Château Margaux. Among other châteaux bringing honor to the small Margaux appellation are Angludet, Giscours, du Tertre, Palmer, Prieuré-Lichine, La Tour de Mons, Monbrison, Malescot-St.- Exupéry, Rausan-Ségla and Brane-Cantenac.

✦ **HAUT MÉDOC:** In the same area as the famous Bordeaux towns, the Haut Médoc region is a large appellation that produces many fine wines of outstanding value. The top name is La Lagune, followed by Cantemerle, Camensac and Château Citran.

✦ **MÉDOC:** Located in the northern area once known as the Bas Médoc, this region supplies many pleasant, early-maturing Clarets. La Tour de By, Plagnac, La Cardonne and Moulin Rouge provide quality wines to enjoy while prize vintages remain in the cellar.

♦ **St. Emilion:** Overall, the large St. Emilion region is responsible for most of the great values from Bordeaux. The typical version blends Merlot and Cabernet Franc grapes with a dollop of Cabernet Sauvignon. Not abrasively tannic, St. Emilion wines are enjoyable when young. Figeac and Cheval Blanc are famous and priced accordingly; more price-sensitive are L'Angèlus, Beauséjour-Bécot, Canon, Canon La Gaffelière, Pavie Decesse, and Grand-Pontet.

♦ **Pessac-Léognan (Graves):** Home to Haut-Brion and La Mission Haut-Brion, Graves is located south of Bordeaux and yields many good to excellent wines, both red and white. For the reds, renewed enthusiasm is being directed toward Pape-Clément, De Fieuzal, Domaine de Chevalier, La Tour-Martillac, Haut-Bailly and La Louvière, exciting in 1988 and '89.

♦ **Pomerol:** Made famous by Château Pétrus, Pomerol is a small appellation adjacent to St. Emilion. The soft, round Merlot grape figures prominently in Pomerol's wines, which have enjoyed unusually strong demand in the 1980s. Along with Pétrus are Lafleur, Vieux Château Certan, Clinet, Certan de May, Lagrange, de Sales, Le Pin, Le Bon Pasteur and Clos René.

White Bordeaux

BEGINNING WHERE THE MEDOC ENDS IN THE SOUTH, the Graves district is a major producer of white wines as well as reds. The whites from Bordeaux are composed of Sauvignon Blanc, which supplies aroma and acidity, over Semillon, which contributes body and texture. When used, Muscadelle adds fragrance.

♦ **Pessac-Léognan (Graves):** This newly created appellation was carved out of Graves and contains most of the famous estates. Recently great strides have been made by two historic names, Château Carbonnieux and Domaine de Chevalier. Other well-balanced white wines come from Malartic-Lagravière, Olivier, La Louvière, Couhins-Lurton and de Cruzeau. Château Haut-Brion and Château Laville-Haut-Brion are two rare whites deserving separate mention.

♦ **Graves:** Still a widely used appellation, Graves are medium-bodied and dry, with average aging potential. Among the most consistent producers are the châteaux of La Tour-Martillac and De Fieuzal.

♦ **Entre-Deux-Mers:** Light, crisp and refreshing are typical characteristics of the new and improved white wines under this name. Most of what is sold as "Bordeaux Blanc" has been redefined as Entre-Deux-Mers.

FROM
CÔTE-TO-COAST
BOUCHARD PÈRE & FILS

Domaines du Château de Beaune

Beaune du Château *Premier Cru*
*Beaune *"Clos de la Mousse"*
*Beaune *"Clos Saint-Landry"*
*Beaune-Grèves *Vigne de L'Enfant Jésus*
Beaune-*"Marconnets"*
Beaune-*"Teurons"*
Chambertin
Chambolle-Musigny
Chevalier-Montrachet
Corton-Charlemagne
Le Corton
Meursault-*"Genevrières"*
Montrachet
Pommard *Premier Cru*
Savigny-Les-Beaune *"Les Lavières"*
Volnay-*"Caillerets"*
Volnay-*"Chanlin"*
*Volnay-Fremiets *"Clos de la Rougeotte"*
Volnay-*"Taillepieds"*

Fine Burgundy and Rhône Wines from Bouchard Père Et Fils

"Le Chamville" Beaujolais-Villages
"Le Chamville" Macon-Villages
*Château De La Font Du Loupe
   Châteauneuf-du-Pape

*Depuis 1731 - Au Château -
Beaune - Côte-D'Or - France*

*Sole Proprietor

BURGUNDY (BOURGOGNE)

EVEN THOUGH ITS SOILS ARE POOR, the beautiful Burgundy wine region produces great wines. The famous vineyards climb steep slopes rich in chalk and limestone. Known as the "Côte d'Or," these slopes consist of the Côte de Nuits in the north and the Côte de Beaune in the south, where Pinot Noir is coaxed into fabled red wines and Chardonnay into treasured whites. Vintages vary in quality, especially for reds, and most Burgundies are in short supply.

WHITE BURGUNDY

♦ **CHABLIS:** Though the name "Chablis" appears on wines made elsewhere, Chablis itself is a cozy village that produces only white wines from Chardonnay. Quality Chablis is soft in texture yet brisk in acidity, with an aroma of apples and minerals and a hint of butter in the background. The wines are identified by four appellations, which, in descending order of prestige, are Grand Cru, Premier Cru, Chablis and Petit Chablis. The virtues of Chablis are most evident in Grand Cru and Premier Cru. Names with a proven record are Domaine Laroche, William Fèvre, Dauvissat, Raveneau, Baron Patrick and Simmonet-Fèbre.

♦ **MEURSAULT:** By Burgundy's standards, Meursault is a large region. Best known for its white wines labeled Meursault or Meursault Premier Cru, the region produces a wine with a clove-like spice flavor and a lemony, fruity background. The wines are solid, medium-full-bodied with lively acidity. The best age for a decade or more. Producers include Comtes Lafon, Louis Jadot, François Jobard, Michelot, J. Matrot and Leroy.

♦ **MONTRACHET:** Tiny Montrachet became so famous that its two villages, Puligny and Chassagne, changed their names to Puligny-Montrachet and Chassagne-Montrachet. Chassagne-Montrachet and its Premier Cru namesakes are characteristically soft and buttery smooth. Puligny-Montrachet and its Premier Crus are bigger and bolder. Both are top-ranked white wines for aging ability, with those simply called "Montrachet" heading the list. ♦ For first-class Puligny-Montrachet, look for vintages from Louis Latour, Leroy, Louis Jadot, Bouchard (Domaine de Château de Beaune), Domaine Leflaive, Michel Colin, Joseph Drouhin and Olivier Leflaive. Chassagne-Montrachet leaders are Bachelet-Ramonet, Marquis de Laguiche, Louis Latour, F. Coffinet, B. Morey, Domaine Duc de Magenta and Joseph Drouhin.

♦ **ALOXE CORTON:** This simple village is home to what many maintain is the greatest, longest-lived white burgundy of all, Corton-Charlemagne. The wines are honeyed, spicy and exotically scented, with enough depth to justify the expense. Louis Latour's version is often exquisite, as are those by Faiveley, Tollot-Beaut & Fils and Domaine Bonneau de Martray.

♦ **GEVREY-CHAMBERTIN:** This tiny village claims two of the world's most collectible reds, Chambertin and Chambertin Clos de Bez, both of Grand Cru status. Here, the Pinot Noir grape reveals its plum and cherry fragrance in a solid, medium-bodied package. Producers maintaining the region's highest standards include Latour, Faiveley, Joseph Drouhin, Ponsot, Rossignol, Leclerc, Jadot, Mugneret and Grivelet.

♦ **MOREY-SAINT-DENIS:** Morey-Saint-Denis makes several famous wines, among them the single-vineyard wines of "Clos de Tart," "Clos de Lambrays," "Clos Saint Denis," "Clos de la Roche" and "Bonnes Mares." Characterized by a peppery, earthy component, they have a wonderful velvety texture. Present leaders include the fabled Comte de Vogüé, Domaine Dujac, Domain Ponsot, Drouhin and Faiveley.

♦ **CHAMBOLLE MUSIGNY:** At their best, wines from this village are considered to be the most delicate, silky and subtle of all fine red Burgundy. The two famous single vineyards are "Musigny" and "Bonnes Mares." Currently upholding the standards are Comte de Vogüé, Daniel Rion, Jadot, Georges Mugneret, Château de Chambolle-Musigny and Roumier.

♦ **VOUGEOT:** The large Clos de Vougeot is the name here, but because the vineyard is big, many producers offer wine labeled "Clos de Vougeot." Among the best are Daniel Rion, Bichot, Joseph Drouhin and René Engel.

♦ **ECHÉZEAUX:** If this town's name were easier for English-speakers to pronounce, its wines would be better known and higher priced. The Pinot Noir develops plummy fruit and complexity, and the best wines mature early. Look for Drouhin, Georges Mugneret, Bichot and Chauvenet.

♦ **VOSNE-ROMANÉE:** This village would be better known if it were not dominated by one producer, the Domaine de la Romanée Conti. Within the village are seven Grand Cru wines: La Romanée, La Romanée-Conti, La Tâche, Richebourg, Romanée-Saint Vivant, Echézeaux and Grand-Echézeaux. The Grand Crus do not have to reveal which village they call home, which explains why Vosne Romanée remains a sleeper. However, wines identified as Vosne Romanée from the following producers should not disappoint: Meo-Camuzet, Jean Gros, Henri Jayer, Bouchard Père & Fils, Georges Mugneret and Jean Grivot.

♦ **NUITS ST. GEORGES:** An appellation that currently stands out for early-maturing wines, Nuits St. Georges is a good choice in restaurants and is reasonably priced. These producers have worked hard to re-establish the region: Daniel Rion, Robert Chevillon, Lupé-Cholet and Méo-Camuzet.

♦ **VOLNAY:** Volnay delivers good-to-exciting red wines to enjoy this decade. The pacesetters are the Domaine des Comtes Lafon, Bouchard Père et Fils (Domaine de Château de Beaune), Domaine de la Pousse d'Or, Michel Lafarge and Domaine Marquis d'Angerville.

THE RHONE VALLEY

A ONCE NEGLECTED REGION IN SOUTHEASTERN FRANCE, the Rhône Valley soared to the top of the wine world thanks to the per-fumed, fragrant, full-flavored red wines made to varying degrees from the Syrah grape. The region is divided into the Northern Rhône, home to several majestic but small appellations, and the Southern Rhône, larger and known for Châteauneuf-du-Pape.

♦ **COTE ROTIE:** The red wines from the Côte Rôtie, or "roasted slopes," reflect the richness and warmth of the area. Smelling of cassis, berries and wildflowers, the wines are great companions to highly seasoned foods and can age for several decades. The leading producers of this splendid wine are Guigal, Jaboulet, Rostaing, Jasmin, Châpoutier and Drevon.

♦ **HERMITAGE:** Called the "manliest red wine of France," Hermitage is indeed a muscular wine that many connoisseurs rank among the greatest. Though some white wine is made, the reds are in demand, especially those by Paul Jaboulet (La Chapelle), Chave, Châpoutier, Guigal and Sorrel.

♦ **CORNAS:** A small, 230-acre appellation, Cornas can be a great, less expen-sive alternative to Hermitage. In outstanding vintages, Cornas competes with its Rhône neighbors and delights its followers. Highly recommended are Marcel Juge, Auguste Clape and Jaboulet.

♦ **CHATEAUNEUF-DU-PAPE:** Wonderfully diverse and often exciting, Southern Rhône wines are a blend of Grenache, Syrah and eleven other possibilities. The best wines are soft and generous, with an inviting straw-berry, spicy, peppery character. After Beaujolais, Châteauneuf-du-Pape is the most versatile food companion. Leaders are Vieux Télégraphe and Beaucastel; Guigal, Fortia, Deydier, Paul Jaboulet, Mont-Olivet, Pignan-Château Reyas, Font du Michelle and Mont Redon are also excellent.

♦ **CONDRIEU:** Almost legendary, Condrieu is a small appellation that yields magnificent white wines. It also contains a seven-acre independent appel-lation that is so famous the wines are identified by its one producer, Château Grillet. The Condrieu white grape is the Viognier, which imparts an aroma of honeysuckle and ripe pears, with hints of honey and wildflow-ers. Condrieu is a massive white wine capable of aging for five to eight years. The following are available in the United States: Georges Vernay, Delas Frères, Etienne Guigal and du Rozay.

♦ **CHATEAU GRILLET:** Made from 100 percent Viognier, this wine from the smallest registered appellation in the world became famous because it was so scarce. Today, it is still wonderful in some vintages.

de Ladoucette

Quite simply, the ultimate Pouilly-Fumé

LOIRE VALLEY

RUNNING SOME 600 MILES FROM EAST TO WEST, the Loire River traverses some of the most beautiful châteaux and wine country in all of France. Many of the wine estates are small in output and sell locally. The types of wine are surprisingly diverse, but the majority are white, with Rosé and sparkling wine both enjoying considerable success in the area.

- **SANCERRE:** In the eastern Loire, Sancerre is close to Pouilly-Fumé, and both regions favor the Sauvignon Blanc for white wines. Sancerre wines are usually medium-bodied and tart, with extremely lively acidity. One of the standout producers is Paul Cotat, whose Sancerre "Chavignol" wines are fragrant and steely. Other fine producers of Sancerre are Château du Nozay, Vacheron, Lucien Thomas Archambault and P. Jolivet.

- **POUILLY-FUMÉ:** The La Doucette name, which now dominates both production and quality, made Pouilly-Fumé famous. Often razor-sharp, the wines are very pungent in aroma, perfect with thick cheeses. They can also be aged for four to five years. The Masson-Blondelet name offers superb wines, as do Châtelain, Pascal, Jolivet and Castelac.

- **VOUVRAY:** In the central part of the Loire, Vouvray is one of the most recognized Loire wines. The widely planted grape here is Chenin Blanc. The appellation allows for the making of both sparkling and non-sparkling wine, though Vouvray is generally regarded as non-sparkling. Both sweet and tart in the aftertaste, the typical Vouvray is a delightful match for many lightly seasoned dishes. For years, the Château de Moncontour has been the most widely enjoyed Vouvray; Marc Bredif is another reliable brand, along with Foreau, M. Martin and R. Loyau.

- **COTEAUX DU LAYON:** An unusual sweet style that rarely leaves France, Coteaux de Layon is produced from Chenin Blanc grapes. But its distinctive style manifests itself through the appearance of the noble rot, *Botrytis cinerea*, for a wine scented of honey and spices. More powerful than a late harvest wine, it is not as rich and heavy as a Sauternes. One producer who sends us a few cases is Domaine Beaujeau.

- **MUSCADET:** A large region in the western Loire, Muscadet is extremely cool. Originally from Burgundy, the grape that adapted well to the climate is now known as either the Melon or Muscadet variety. Widely available, Muscadets are dry, crisp and light- to medium-bodied. Though not wines to cellar, they are sturdy and complement shellfish beautifully. Those labeled "*Sur Lie*" were aged in contact with their yeast cells to acquire more flavors and soften their acidity. Standouts are the Château du Cléray, Domaine Quilla, Meurgey and Domaine de la Batarvière.

*I'll·be crushed if I don't get picked
by Laurent-Perrier.*

You'll be crushed if you do.

Grand Siècle Champagne

From Laurent-Perrier

CHAMPAGNE

IN THE NORTHEAST CORNER OF FRANCE, Champagne is the coolest wine region and has a late, often difficult harvest. Blended from three grapes, Chardonnay, Pinot Noir and Pinot Meunier, Champagne ages in the bottle along with the yeast cells that help develop its complex character. ✦ Champagne's degree of yeasty-toasty character, body (or weight) and relative dryness varies from producer to producer. Each strives for individuality — a "House Style." When the wine is properly chilled, Champagne bubbles should be tiny but very active. ✦ Champagnes are more compatible with meals than once thought, but one must sample a range to find the perfect match. "Brut" is a popular style that's generally not sweet; "Extra Dry" is sweeter than Brut.

✦ **NON-VINTAGE BRUT:** The majority of Champagne is non-vintage, meaning a blend of wines made in two or more years. The master blend, known as the cuvée, is aged an average of three years, ready to enjoy by consumers without additional aging. Like all fine Champagne, it is best served chilled in a tulip or flute-shaped glass. The leading names in the Brut category are Krug, Moët et Chandon, Piper Heidsieck, Laurent Perrier, Bollinger Special Cuvée, Charles Heidsieck Reserve, Veuve Clicquot, Gosset, Mumm Cordon Rouge, Pol Roger, Roederer, Taittinger and Perrier-Jouët.

✦ **VINTAGE BRUT:** Produced in small quantities, Vintage Champagne generates the most excitement. Made only in the occasional outstanding vintage, it is then given extra-special aging (five years or more) by the producer. The best represent the highest sensory reward mere grapes can bestow. Among the many fine Vintage Champagnes are those made by Krug, Bollinger "Grand Année," Clicquot "La Grande Dame," Mumm "René Lalou," Perrier-Jouët "Fleur de Champagne," Laurent Perrier "Grand Siècle," Piper Heidsieck "Rare," Philipponnat "Clos des Goisses," Cristal, and the grand-daddy of them all, Dom Pérignon.

✦ **ROSÉ CHAMPAGNE:** Whether vintage or not, Rosé Champagne became the hit bubbly of the 1980s. The delightful russet-pink tint emanates from greater use of red grapes in the cuvée. Most Rosés offer more depth of flavor and a richer body than other Champagnes. As a result, they can be enjoyed with many entrées as well as appetizers. More and more producers are adding a Rosé to their line. For now, try Dom Pérignon, Krug, Clicquot, Billecart-Salmon, Bollinger "Grande Année Rosé" and Taittinger "Comtes des Champagnes."

BAROLO & PIEDMONT WINES

FROM THE PIEDMONT DISTRICT SOUTH OF ALBA comes one of the world's most powerful and long-lived red wines, Barolo. Historians call Barolo the "wine of kings, and the king of wines." It takes its name from the village of Barolo and is made from the Nebbiolo variety, a highly sensitive grape that develops well along the hillsides. Barolo has enchanting, contrasting aromas of truffles and roses, tar and spices. An acquired taste, fine Barolo is big, robust and strong in alcohol, with a degree of woodiness after long aging. Like many great wines, it is made in small quantities: only 3,000 acres comprise the delimited area. The Nebbiolo makes many other red wines in neighboring sectors of Piedmont, and they too are presented here.

♦ **BAROLO:** To qualify for the name, a Barolo must be given at least three years of aging, two in barrel. A Barolo Riserva is aged for a minimum of five years, two in barrel, before it is sold. A Riserva often needs years, even decades, of aging to reach its prime. Among the leaders are Ceretto, Aldo Conterno, Giacosa, Vietti, Prunotto, Pio Cesare, Mascarello and Fontanafredda. Today, the most exciting Barolos are the single-vineyard versions, especially those by Ceretto called "Bricco Rocche" and "Prapo Bricco Rocche."

♦ **BARBARESCO:** Just east of Alba, the town of Barbaresco is well regarded for its red wine made from Nebbiolo. The regular bottlings are aged at least two years, and the Riservas must be held for four. The single-vineyard wines from Gaja called "Sori Tildin" and "Sori San Lorenzo" are remarkable. "Bricco Asili" is the outstanding wine from Ceretto. Other worthwhile Barbarescos are Prunotto, "Asij" from Ceretto, Castello di Neive and Bruno Giacosa, especially his "Santo Stefano de Neive Riserva."

♦ **DOLCETTO:** "Dolcetto" means sweet, but this Piedmont wine is medium-bodied and dry. The best versions offer an exquisite aroma of strawberries and cherries, with a refreshing acidity and moderate tannins. One of the finest is by Marcarini, with its "Bochi di Berry" special batch made from ancient vines. Other first-rate producers are Giacosa, Mascarrello, Clerico, Vietti and Bel Colle.

♦ **NEBBIOLO D'ALBA:** Similar to Barbaresco, Nebbiolo d'Alba is somewhat more variable in quality. Originating from vineyards surrounding Alba that are outside of both Barolo and Barbaresco, it reaches maturity sooner than Barolo, yet still offers richness and complexity. Leading producers include Angelo Gaja, Bruno Giacosa, Scarpa, Alfredo Prunotto, Fontanafredda, Mascarello and Ceretto.

If Château Latour '61 is just another bottle of wine,

then The Glendronach is just another bottle of Scotch.

In the renowned wine region of Bordeaux, France you can find some of the world's most famous châteaux. Though they may share the same geographical appellation, to the experienced wine connoisseur their subtle differences give them each a distinct character.

The same thing can be said of the world's finest single malt Scotches. Nestled in the romantic Scottish Highlands you'll find The Glendronach, perhaps the most exquisite of all single malts.

The differences between The Glendronach and the other comparable single malt Scotches are attributed to centuries-old distilling methods. And The Glendronach offers a rare single malt that's patiently aged for 12 years in oaken sherry casks, which impart a unique, well-rounded, subtle flavour, rich colour and smooth texture.

To some, the differences may be subtle, but to a connoisseur's taste, it makes all the difference in the world — and well worth its higher price.

The GLENDRONACH
Very Rare Single Highland Malt Scotch

BRUNELLO DI MONTALCINO
& OTHER ITALIAN RED WINES

BRUNELLO, SAID TO BE A SPECIAL VARIANT of Sangiovese, the Chianti grape, flourishes in the village of Montalcino in southern Tuscany. This rich and long-lived wine is famous thanks to the Biondi-Santi family, developers of the special grape in the 1880s and for years the only major producer. Other companies have developed vineyards around Montalcino, including Banfi with its magnificent Castello Banfi, and just over 2,000 acres are now planted. ♦ The regulations governing Brunello production state that it must be given a minimum of four years aging prior to release, and it must be barrel- or wood-aged for three and a half. An alternative designation, Rosso di Montalcino, was established for wines that were not aged in wood for any set minimum. Of late, these fruitier wines have found a niche in the market.

♦ **BRUNELLO DI MONTALCINO:** Powerful and compact, Brunello wines offer berries and spice along with leathery, earthy components. They can be extremely astringent when young and need cellaring for at least ten years. Biondi-Santi reigns supreme, but the competition includes Banfi, San Felice, Col d'Orcia, Il Greppone Mazzi and Caparzo.

♦ **ROSSO DI MONTALCINO:** Some Americans prefer this to Brunello. The plummy fruit and richness is unencumbered by wood, but there's plenty of tannin for aging at least five years. Both Caparzo and Banfi make excellent versions, as do Col d'Orcia and Biondi-Santi.

♦ **SASSICAIA:** From the outskirts of Tuscany near Bolgheri comes a red wine that enjoys a fanatic cult following, Sassicaia. Made from Cabernet Sauvignon and Cabernet Franc, it is produced by Tenuta San Guido and was among the first Italian wines to truly resemble a first-class Bordeaux.

♦ **AMARONE:** Amarone is a special red wine made near Verona in the Valpolicella district. Incredibly powerful and exotically scented, it is made by selecting very ripe grapes that are dried on trays for three months to concentrate their flavor. The wine is not actually made until late January of the following year. Masi offers classic Amarone.

♦ **TAURASI:** An extraordinary wine that seems to age for decades, Taurasi is made from an ancient grape variety, the Aglianico. It responds magically to the conditions in and around Avelino, which is in the south in Campania. The village of Taurasi is represented by the Mastroberardinos, a great wine-producing family.

MOLTO
CERETTO

STILE
QUALITÀ
MODERNO
ITALIANO

CERETTO
CARNEIS

B
LANGE'

onchera

1984

CERETTO

Produce ed affina vini del Piemonte in Alba

BARBARESCO

Denominazione di origine controllata
e garantita

ETICHETTE DISEGNATE DA *SILVIO COPPOLA*, MILANO

Registro imbott. 8671 CN - Imbott

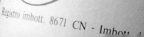

CHIANTI & PROPRIETARY REDS

ONE OF THE OLDEST AND BEST-KNOWN WINES, Chianti has recently been in a state of flux. The leaders in Tuscany are redesigning their famous wine, hoping to bury its image as a cheap carafe wine in a straw-wrapped bottle. In 1984, they took the first step and changed the regulations to allow producers to use better-suited grapes and more red than white varieties. ◆ Chianti is already new and improved, and since the Tuscan hills yield around ten million cases annually, there's plenty to go around.

◆ **CHIANTI:** Wine simply labeled "Chianti" tends to be the lightest in style. Intended to be enjoyed in its youth, this style of Chianti is the most popular wine in the many fine restaurants of Florence. Several well-established producers do send some here, including the leaders, Frescabaldi and Barone Ricasoli, as well as Rampolla, Gabbiano and Pasolini.

◆ **CHIANTI CLASSICO:** This designation applies to wines produced in the official "inner zone" between Siena and Florence. Typically full-flavored yet balanced, Classico wines have berries, spice and an occasional leathery component in the aroma. To protect the region's reputation, producers formed an association that uses the black rooster as its symbol. About one-third of all Chianti is Classico, and the greatest improvements are apparent in its bottlings. Among the best are Antinori, Castello del Rampolla, Isole E Olena, Lilliano, Castello di Volpaia and Villa Caffaggio.

◆ **CHIANTI CLASSICO RISERVA:** When the wines are aged three years or more by the producer, they earn the designation "Riserva." Aging can be either in barrels or bottles, so the style of the final wine varies widely. Usually the pride of the house, Riservas are the best Chiantis for aging. "Ducale" from Ruffino is famous, as are Antinori's and Villa Banfi's. Others to look for are Isole E Olena, Il Paggio, Castello di Abolo, Castello del Rampolla, Castello di Querceto, San Felice, Monsanto, Cispiano, Melini, Nozzole, La Massa, Ricasoli Fossi and Il Poggiolino.

◆ **VINO DA TAVOLA:** This lowly sounding designation means "table wine," but it often appears on wines that are creative and profoundly exciting. Part of the new wave of Italian reds, they are usually produced in Tuscany and Piedmont, using grapes and combinations not permitted for their appellations but capable of greatness nonetheless. Unable to label them by their place names, producers create proprietary names, such as Antinori's 1971 renegade blend, Tignanello. Other new-wave, truly exciting reds to look for are Solaia (Antinori), Campofiorin (Masi), Tinscvil (Monsanto), Cabreo (Ruffino), Vigorello (San Felice) and Sammarco (di Rampolla).

ITALIAN WHITE WINES

UPGRADING ITALIAN WHITE WINES to make them equal to the reds while appealing to current taste preferences has demanded a recent outpouring of money and effort. Once-proud vineyards are switching to such varieties as Chardonnay and Sauvignon Blanc, while old-fashioned white grapes such as Trebbiano are disappearing. The new-wave Italian whites have varietal designations that simplify marketing — sometimes the special blends even carry made-up proprietary names. Today, two regions enjoying particular success with white wines are located in the north: Trentino-Alto Adige and Friuli. Other new-wave whites are coming from Tuscany and Piedmont.

* **PINOT GRIGIO:** A pleasantly fruity, spicy white wine, Pinot Grigio is coming into its own. It is medium- to light-bodied with good, snappy acidity. Some of the best producers include Brigil in the Alto Adige, Boscaini, Plozner, La Viarte and Tieffenbrunner. Banfi subtitles its lovely Pinot Grigio "San Angelo."

* **ARNEIS:** Made in Piedmont from Arneis grapes, this is a distinctive light, fruity wine with a slight spritz. Two important producers are Ceretto ("Blange") and Giacosa.

* **CHARDONNAY:** Because Italian vintners want to show their oenological abilities to the world, they are working to style Chardonnay like a Meursault or a Napa Valley barrel-aged version. Among the pioneers are Gaja's full-bodied Chardonnay from Piedmont, Banfi's impressive "Fontanelle," and Santa Margarita, with vineyards in Alto Adige. Another major player is Avbignones's "Il Marzocco."

* **ORVIETO:** From Umbria comes Orvieto, a blend of several varieties. Uneven in quality until the early 1980s, it has been coming on strong in recent years. The most consistent are those labeled "Classico." Quality-minded producers include Barbi, Antinori, Barberani, Bigi and Melini.

* **SOAVE:** As the most popular white export, Soave can make a pleasant companion. Several producers in Veneto are working hard to give it more character. They include Pieropan, Anselmi and Masi.

* **PROPRIETARY WHITES:** The ubiquitous Antinori family makes the lovely "Galestro," a blend of Sauvignon Blanc and Procanico. "Libaio" is a terrific white wine from the house of Ruffino that blends Chardonnay with Sauvignon Blanc. Introduced by Brolio Ricasoli, "Nebbiano" is a light, lively white wine made from Sauvignon Blanc and the Italian Riesling. "Terre Alte" from Livio Felluga is a classic white wine blended from Toscai, Sauvignon Blanc and Pinot Blanco grapes.

To improve this meal, just add water.

The perfect accompaniment to an exquisite meal is an equally exquisite beverage. Quite naturally, we recommend Evian, from the French Alps.

Evian's purity makes it clear, light, and refreshing. Which means it will make a delightful complement to any meal at any time. And it has the wonderful ability to cleanse the palate between courses, and wines.

Besides, Evian is natural spring water without bubbles. So you won't feel filled up when you drink it.

That's why, if good food graces your table, so should Evian.

EVIAN. THE BALANCE.™

BOTTLED WATERS

BY ARTHUR VON WIESENBERGER

*I*N 1990 ALONE, MORE THAN TWO BILLION GALLONS of bottled water were sold, making water the best-selling beverage in the United States. Both domestic and imported spring waters have become an integral part of fine dining, offering a refreshing alternative to tap water and soft drinks. ♦ Every spring is as unique as a fingerprint, with its own composition of minerals, trace elements and, in some cases, natural carbonation. In Europe, bottled waters are believed to enhance health. Some bottled waters have considerable natural bicarbonates, which are stimulating to the digestive system. In the United States, bottled waters are not sold for health benefits, but for flavor. ♦ Bottled water should be served chilled, without ice. Carbonated waters are a superb natural mixer with fruit juices, wine or spirits, while non-carbonated waters are ideal food companions.

♦ **APOLLINARIS MINERAL WATER:** Apollinaris has been bottled since 1852 in the Ahr Valley of Germany. Aggressive carbonation, high mineralization and exceptional bicarbonates make it a good digestive stimulant.

♦ **ARROWHEAD MOUNTAIN SPRING WATER:** First bottled in 1894, Arrowhead Spring comes from California. Lightly mineralized, this water is available in California and Arizona in still and carbonated versions or with added flavors.

♦ **CALISTOGA SPARKLING MINERAL WATER:** Natural geyser water has been bottled in the historic spa town of Calistoga since 1924. The water surfaces at boiling point and is then cooled and carbonated. It is sold throughout the West plain, flavored or mixed with juices.

♦ **CRYSTAL GEYSER SPARKLING MINERAL WATER:** Bottled since 1978 at the Calistoga site where it is cooled and carbonated, Crystal Geyser's moderate carbonation and mineralization have made this thermal spring water a winner at numerous tastings. Water with added flavors and fruit juices, and a recently introduced non-carbonated, Sierra alpine spring water are also favorites.

◆**EVIAN NATURAL SPRING WATER:** Discovered in 1789, Evian was first bottled in 1826 by the Dukes of Savoy. Snow and rain filter through the slopes of the northern French Alps to the Source Cachat in the town of Evian-les-Bains. The water is lightly mineralized and non-carbonated.

◆ **FERRARELLE NATURALLY SPARKLING MINERAL WATER:** Ferrarelle comes from moderately mineralized, naturally carbonated springs north of Naples, Italy. Known since Pliny the Elder praised the waters of the Assano Valley, it was first bottled in 1893.

◆**HENNIEZ:** Henniez spring was discovered by the Romans in the valley of the Broye in Switzerland and is said to have been visited by Napoleon. First bottled in 1905, both the moderately carbonated and non-carbonated Henniez waters are imported to the United States. Mildly mineralized, it is also sold in flavors.

◆**LA CROIX:** La Croix was one of the first domestic bottled waters to be served in flight, by United Airlines. Bottled by the G. Heileman Brewing Company since 1980, the water is carbon-filtered and carbonated.

◆**LEVISSIMA:** From a spring in the Italian Alps near Lake Como, Levissima is a mineralized calcium bicarbonate water. It comes in non-carbonated, carbonated and lightly carbonated versions.

◆**MENDOCINO MINERAL WATER:** Mendocino has been bottled at the source since 1880. Naturally carbonated and highly mineralized, it has an exceptional level of calcium bicarbonate.

◆**MOUNTAIN VALLEY SPRING WATER:** From a spring near Hot Springs, Arkansas, Mountain Valley has been bottled since 1871. It is a non-carbonated, highly mineralized water.

◆**PERRIER:** In 1863, Emperor Napoleon III decreed that Perrier's waters should be bottled "for the good of France." Naturally carbonated, the water is also available as Perrier with a Twist, with fruit flavor essences.

◆**QUIBELL MINERAL WATER:** From Sweet Spring Mountain, Quibell has been bottled since 1987, with added carbonation.

◆**RAMLOSA:** Dr. Johan Jacob Dobelius discovered Ramlosa Springs near Helsingborg, Sweden, in 1701. Moderately carbonated and mineralized, it is a favorite of the King of Sweden and the Queen of Denmark.

◆**SAN PELLEGRINO:** San Pellegrino has been bottled in Italy since 1899 and is moderately mineralized and lightly carbonated. Praised for its pleasing taste and small bubbles, it is used by Italians for digestive disorders.

◆**SARATOGA SPARKLING MINERAL WATER:** Famous since the 1890s, Saratoga is bottled with natural, medium carbonation. An elegant bottle and light mineralization add to its appeal.

◆**SPA REINE:** Discovered by the Romans, Spa Reine was first bottled in 1583. This lightly mineralized water is bottled in carbonated and non-carbonated forms and sold in the eastern states.

◆**VITTEL GRANDE SOURCE:** Vittel is a moderately mineralized, non-carbonated water from the Vosges Mountains in northeastern France. It is renowned in France for its stimulation of the kidneys, and the Vittel spa at the source has a popular rejuvenation program.

◆**VOLVIC:** From the heart of the Auvergne Mountains in central France comes Volvic. Discovered in 1927, this lightly mineralized, non-carbonated water is sweet and thirst-quenching.

Arthur von Wiesenberger is the author of numerous books on bottled water. His most recent is THE POCKET GUIDE TO BOTTLED WATERS (CONTEMPORARY BOOKS, 1991).

PEOPLE HAVE BEEN ASKING FOR PERRIER EVER SINCE OUR FIRST AD RAN.

The year was one million twenty four B.C. Man had just developed the art of communication. And, in a land we now call France, he discovered a spring we now call Perrier.

It was clear and pure and sparkling. And so, word of its qualities quickly spread.

Since then, entire civilizations have come and gone, but the source remains. Still yielding water for modern man to drink. Still as pure as the day it was new.

Because, unlike other beverages, it doesn't rely on artificial sweeteners and coloring. Nor does it have caffeine, sugar or even calories.

However, there is a change we would like to point out. The little green bottles Perrier now comes in.

Which is a refreshing change, indeed. Because instead of having to travel to the spring, the spring can now travel to you.

EARTH'S FIRST SOFT DRINK.

What could be even more wonderful than a Jameson Irish Coffee?

A Jameson.

Jameson® is smoother than Scotch. It's lighter than Bourbon. No wonder. It's made from the finest barley and the purest water. But even so, the exquisite, distinct taste of Jameson imported premium whiskey is often hidden in coffee.

So next time, enjoy the unique taste of Jameson on the rocks, with a splash or tall with soda. Just tell your bartender, "Give me an Irish Coffee. Hold the coffee. Hold the cream. Hold the sugar. And pour the Jameson." Enjoy.

Give me a Jameson. Hold the coffee.

SPIRITS & LIQUEURS

BY GERALD D. BOYD

Drink Less, But Drink The Very Best

TODAY'S EMPHASIS ON MODERATE DRINKING is a challenge to be more creative and versatile in what we consume. Spirits & liqueurs come in so many varieties, styles and flavors that they more than meet this challenge. As you discover the many ways to use them in food and drink recipes, you will begin to appreciate higher-quality products. There are degrees of excellence, whether you're buying aged rums, single malt scotches, flavored vodkas or imported liqueurs, and subtle differences among the best brands. What you prefer is a matter of taste, but quality should be the first criterion.

WHISKEY

WHISKEY, SPELLED "WHISKY" by Scots and Canadians, is by definition a "brown spirit," distilled from a select recipe (often called a mash bill) of grains. Whiskeys differ in many subtle ways, but the two major distinctions are determined by the type of still used and the grains in the recipe.

Single malt scotch is an example of whiskey made from one grain, in this case barley, produced in small batches in a pot still. Irish whiskey is also made in a pot still, but the grain recipe may include small quantities of oats, rye and wheat.

Among the best-known Irish whiskeys are Old Bushmills and Jameson. Black Bush, distilled by Bushmills, has more malt whiskey in the blend, making it closer to a single malt.

Scottish immigrants built the Canadian whiskey business, although the Canadian whiskey of today bears little resemblance to Scotch whiskey. Often referred to as "rye," Canadian whiskey is made from cereal grains, primarily corn, with about 10 percent rye and a little barley added to the blend. All Canadian whiskeys are blends and are made in continuous stills. Among the most popular are Canadian Club, Crown Royal, Seagram's V.O., Lord Calvert, Black Velvet, Schenley OFC and Windsor Supreme.

Although most American whiskeys are blends, there are also a number of straight whiskeys. The major difference is in the percentages of various grains used (predominantly corn), and how they are

"A taste of Heaven before the trumpets blow."

—Sandy Milne,
Stillman & Resident Sage.

Sandy Milne waxing poetic.

The word "elegant" crops up time and again when experts describe the taste of The Glenlivet® single malt Scotch.

Some say it's brought about by the peculiar shape of our pot stills.

Some say it's the smoke of the peat cut from the nearby Faemussach peat fields.

Our own Sandy Milne insists that it's the water from Josie's Well, flowing as it does down through peat and over Highland granite.

Whatever, the great Sir Walter Scott long ago put on paper that The Glenlivet "...is the only liquor fit for a gentleman..."

We'll not argue with a one of them.

What is a single malt Scotch?

A single malt is Scotch the way it was originally: one single whisky, from one single distillery. Not, like most Scotch today, a blend of many whiskies. The Glenlivet single malt Scotch whisky should therefore be compared to a château-bottled wine. Blended Scotch is more like a mixture of wines from different vineyards.

The Glenlivet.
The Father of All Scotch.

aged. By Federal law, a blended whiskey must contain at least 20 percent 100-proof straight whiskey by volume. Seagram's 7 Crown dominates the field. Also popular are Calvert, Carstairs, Park & Tilford, Schenley Reserve, Antique, Kessler and Four Roses. American blends enjoy a very strong regional brand loyalty.

Straight whiskey cannot be blended with other whiskeys before aging or bottling. Furthermore, the mash bill blend must consist of at least 51 percent of a single grain.

Bourbon is the best-known straight whiskey produced in the United States, usually from 70 percent corn. It is made in a handful of states, but the best bourbons are considered those from Kentucky.

Bourbons must be aged in new charred-oak casks for at least two years, although many are aged longer. "Sour mash" refers to the use of a sour-mash yeasting process, and may or may not appear as a label term. Maker's Mark and Old Fitzgerald add wheat to their mash bill, resulting in a smoother bourbon with greater finesse. Other quality bourbons include Jim Beam, Wild Turkey, Old Grand-Dad, Ancient Age, I.W. Harper, Benchmark, Old Forester and Weller's Special Reserve.

Tennessee whiskey is similar to bourbon, except that it is filtered through sugar-maple charcoal and aged for a minimum of four years to give it a smooth taste. Jack Daniel's is the leader, but George A. Dickel is also a fine Tennessee whiskey.

SCOTCH

TWO TYPES OF SCOTCH WHISKEY are produced: single malt and blended. Single malt scotch is distilled from pure water and malted barley permeated with varying amounts of peat. Malt whiskey, as it is often called, is the true whiskey of Scotland.

Blended scotch, a relatively recent innovation, is a proprietary house blend of a number of different malt whiskeys and a few grain whiskeys. Top blended scotches include Johnnie Walker, Chivas Regal, Dewar's, Cutty Sark, Cluny, Black & White, Pinch, Desmond & Duff, The Famous Grouse, Haig & Haig, J&B Rare, Bell's, Teacher's, Usher's and White Horse.

Of the two scotch whiskeys, malt whiskey is the more interesting because of its stylistic diversity. Its unique character depends on the source of the barley, the malting process, the amount of peat used to fire the ovens that dry the barley, the water source, and the size and shape of the still. Scotland's malt distilleries are located in four major areas: Highland, Lowland, Island and Cambeltown.

♦ HIGHLAND MALTS: *Highland malts, made near the River Spey, are usually well balanced in flavor and body, with a pleasing touch of pungent peat. Quality Highland malts include Cardhu, Glenmorangie, The Macallan, Knockando, Mortlach, Glenfarclas, Glendronach and The Dalmore. The Glenlivet and Glenfiddich, top sellers in the United States, are Highland malts.*

♦ LOWLAND MALTS: *The few Lowland malts made are among the lightest, both in color and flavor, with just a touch of peat. At present, Auchentoshan, Glenkinchie and Rosebank are the most commonly available.*

♦ ISLAND MALTS: *Islay, off the Atlantic coast, produces the most distinctive Island malts. For some malt drinkers, Laphroaig, with its pronounced peat flavor, is the quintessential Islay malt. Less intense, with a little more finesse, are Bunnahabhain, Bruichladdich, Bowmore and Lagavulin.*

♦ CAMBELTOWN MALTS: *Southeast of Islay is Cambeltown, the smallest of the four producing areas. Only Springbank and Glen Scotia continue to distill malt whiskey.*

GIN

ONE OF THE YOUNGEST SPIRITS, gin dates to the mid-seventeenth century. Dr. Sylvius, a Dutch professor of medicine, created gin as an inexpensive diuretic and purifying tonic. He called his tonic *genièvre*, the French word for juniper. The Dutch shortened it to *genever*, which they use today for what we call gin.

To make gin, distillers, following a closely guarded formula, produce a pure neutral spirit from juniper, derived from the berries of evergreen trees. The spirit is then re-distilled in a pot still to add more flavor. Some distillers prefer to hang the flavoring agents, called botanicals, above the alcohol and let the vapors pick up the flavor subtleties as they rise through. Some popular flavoring botanicals are cinnamon, coriander, angelica root, licorice, bitter almonds, and dried orange and lemon.

Gin does not require aging: in fact, you can drink gin the day it was made. Wood-aging for a short period is sometimes used to give gin a light yellow color. These gins are known as golden gins.

♦ LONDON DRY: *The most popular of gins, real London Dry is either made in England or elsewhere under British license. London Dry is known for its dry and tangy fresh juniper flavor. The most popular English-made London Dry gins are Tanqueray, Beefeater and Bombay Dry. Bombay has now entered the super-premium gin market with Bombay Sapphire, named after India's most celebrated jewel. Sapphire has a smooth, complex flavor. Other London Dry gins, made in the United States, include Gordon's, Gilbey's, Calvert, Booth's and Bellows. Seagram's produces a London Extra Dry as well as Burnett's White Satin.*

VODKA

IN RUSSIA, WHERE *ZHIZNENNIA* vodka has been a popular spirit since the fourteenth century, no one would ever think of mixing vodka with anything. The classic Russian way to drink it is ice-cold and straight up — preferably from a bottle that has been frozen in a block of ice. But since the 1940s, vodka has been popular in the U.S. as a cocktail spirit.

Vodka can be made from any material containing starch. Today, mostly corn is used, though potatoes are still used in Poland and Russia. A mash is pressure-cooked, then mixed with water and fermented. Distillation follows in a continuous still at a high proof of 190 to extract maximum flavoring elements. The new spirit is purified by charcoal filtration and bottled.

♦ AMERICAN & ENGLISH VODKA: *U.S. vodka production began when the Smirnoff family, which had established a reputation for charcoal-filtered vodka in their native Russia, fled during the Revolution and set up business in Connecticut. Today, Heublein produces Smirnoff and the super-premium Smirnoff Silver Private Reserve. England has entered this market with Tanqueray Sterling.*

♦ SCANDINAVIAN VODKA: *Traditionally, Eastern Europe is known for the best vodka. In recent years, though, Scandinavian vodkas have come into their own. More neutral than Eastern European vodkas, Scandinavian vodkas have a clean, fresh flavor. The best-selling, and third overall in popularity, is Sweden's classic Absolut. Other popular*

ABSOLUT
PEPPAR
80 PROOF
PEPPER FLAVORED VODKA,
PRODUCED AND BOTTLED IN SWEDEN. 1.0 LITER.
IMPORTED
IMPORTER AND SOLE DISTRIBUTOR FOR THE U.S.
CARILLON IMPORTERS LTD., TEANECK, N.J.
ABSOLUT MARY.
FOR GIFT DELIVERY OF ABSOLUT PEPPAR ANYWHERE, CALL 1-800-CHEER-UP (EXCEPT WHERE PROHIBITED BY LAW)
PEPPER FLAVORED VODKA 80 PROOF/100% GRAIN NEUTRAL SPIRITS (ABSOLUT COUNTRY OF SWEDEN™) © 1988 CARILLON IMPORTERS LTD., TEANECK, N.J.

Scandinavian vodkas include Iceland's Icy, Finlandia from Finland, Denmark's mellow Denaka and Norway's Vikin Fjord.

♦ EASTERN EUROPEAN VODKA: *Polish vodkas have a full, pungent, yet distinctive taste. The most popular vodkas are potato-based Wyborowa and Luksusowa. Also well-liked is Monopolowa by Baczewski. Among Russian vodkas, Stolichnaya is the best-known brand. Now, the popular Stoli has a super-premium mate, Stolichnaya Cristall, a clean, crisp vodka with a velvety taste.*

♦ FLAVORED VODKA: *Long a popular drink in Poland and Russia, flavored vodka recently has become a hot item in the West. Traditional Polish flavored vodka, such as that from Kord Zubrowka, is infused with bison grass, which the Poles claim will give the drinker the strength of a bison. Not quite so potent is yellow-green Stolichnaya Limonnaya. Sweden's Absolut has Peppar, a clear, spicy vodka made from jalapeño pepper and paprika, and Citron, with its clear color and zesty flavor that combines lemon, lime, mandarin orange and grapefruit. Other flavorings include black pepper, honey, cherry, rowanberry, juniper, green walnut and Malaga wine.*

TEQUILA

THE ORIGINS OF TEQUILA can be traced back to the Aztecs, who produced *pulque,* a milky alcoholic beverage made from the agave plant so abundant in rural Mexico. The Spanish, who brought the skill of distillation with them when they conquered Mexico, distilled *pulque* into mezcal, a clear, brandy-like spirit with a strong, earthy, herbal flavor. Eventually, mezcal (or *pulque*; no one is sure which) was refined through distillation into a spirit known today as tequila.

Tequila is made from the blue agave, which may stand ten feet tall, and has a pineapple-shaped heart that can weigh up to 150 pounds. The agave hearts are chopped and steamed into a sweet concentrate, which is fermented about two days.

A double distillation in pot stills follows, producing a raw spirit of about 104 proof. This "white" or "silver" spirit is reduced with water to 80 proof.

♦ GOLD TEQUILA: *"Gold" tequila has been aged in oak casks for nine months or more. Since there is no government control on the aging, the coloring of gold tequila may be hastened by adding caramel.*

♦ ANEJO: *The best tequila is known as anejo, which means "aged." Anejo may rest in oak for three to ten years, until the right character and flavor are achieved. Connoisseurs think nothing of paying the same price for anejo as that asked for a premium Cognac.*

♦ *White (silver) and gold tequilas are available from Herradura, Two Fingers, Don Emilio, Montezuma, Monte Alban, José Cuervo and Sauza. A few of these also market a mezcal. Anejo tequilas are rarer, with one of the best available from Herradura.*

RUM

BORN AS A TONIC to help English settlers cope with the rigors of life in the West Indies, rum, not raw sugar, was the first product of island sugar cane. The name is thought to have come from the English country slang expression "rumbullion," the roaring noise inside the head caused by the drink. Rum became the spirit of the islands by the mid-eighteenth century.

It was perhaps inevitable that rum became the favored drink of the pirates who roamed the Caribbean. The notorious pirate chantey "Fifteen Men on a Dead Man's Chest" had as its refrain, "Yo ho ho and a bottle of rum." The English navy once carried rum among its rations, as it was thought to prevent scurvy; today's rum punch called "grog" gets its name from the daily dose of rum and water administered by the English Admiral nicknamed "Old Grog."

ABSOLUT APPEAL.

Rum is the distillate of fermented molasses, sugar cane syrup and sugar cane juice. A mash is fermented and sent through a continuous or column still. The clear raw spirit is matured and mellowed in small oak casks for six months to twelve years, then bottled at 80 to 90 proof. Although they are made elsewhere, the best rums are from the Caribbean.

Rums are made in two main styles — light and dark. Light rums are perfect for warm-weather fruit-based drinks such as daiquiris and Mai Tais, while dark rums are favored for drinks traditionally served in winter, like eggnog and hot buttered rum. The classic, potent planter's punch, however, could be made with nothing but cool, dark rum. Both styles are refreshing served straight over ice with lime.

♦ LIGHT RUM: *Often labeled "Silver" or "White," light rums are light in body and subtle in flavor. Produced in the islands originally settled by the Spanish, such as Puerto Rico and Cuba, light rums are favored in the United States because they are well suited for mixed drinks.*

Puerto Rico's Bacardi is the top-selling brand in the U.S. Other popular Puerto Rican rums include Ronrico, Ron Castillo, Palo Viejo and Captain Morgan Spiced Rum. Another type of light rum is Demerara, from Guyana. Lemon Hart, Guyana's legendary 151-proof rum, is used in high-octane cocktails like the Zombie.

♦ MEDIUM RUM: *Medium-colored rums stay in the cask for up to three years and get their deep amber hue from the addition of caramel. Usually labeled "Amber" or "Gold," these fuller rums are richer in flavor, sometimes with a little sweetness. Bacardi Gold Reserve from Puerto Rico and Mount Gay and Cockspur are quality medium rums, as are Cruzan, Montego Bay and Old St. Croix from the Virgin Islands.*

♦ DARK RUM: *Less popular, but no less appealing, are the rich, full-bodied dark rums of Jamaica. Made from molasses, with additions from previous distillations, Jamaican rums are round and flavor-packed. The best known are Myers's Jamaican Punch, Appleton and Lemon Hart Jamaica. A new entry into the U.S. rum market is the richly flavored Aniversario from Venezuela's Pampero.*

♦ FRENCH ISLAND RUM: *The so-called French Island rums of Haiti and Martinique have a more refined bouquet and flavor because they are dis-*

tilled from fresh cane juice, not molasses, and are aged, like fine Cognac, in oak casks. Negrita and Clement are Martinique's best-known rums. Haiti's Barbancourt is available in Three Star, Five Star and fifteen-year-old.

SPECIALTY DRINKS

SOME DRINKS CANNOT be placed into any specific category. Vermouth, for example, is not a wine, although it has a wine base. And it is not a liqueur, even though it is flavored. For the sake of simplicity, these in-between spirits belong to the "specialty drinks" group.

With its bittersweet herbal flavor, vermouth is a basic aperitif. The drier white is used alone with a twist or as a mixer for cocktails such as the Martini. Heavier and sweeter, the red is used mostly as an ingredient in such drinks as the Manhattan, although it can stand alone. Notable vermouths include France's Noilly Prat, and Italy's Cinzano and Martini & Rossi.

Most aperitifs, such as the Italian Punt e Mes, are variations on vermouth, wine-based and flavored with herbs and bitter plants. Some believe that bitters are a digestive, a tonic and even an aphrodisiac. Bitters such as Angostura, Underberg and Fernet Branca are well-known as digestives.

Italy's most popular aperitif is Campari. Like all aperitifs, it has a secret recipe of aromatic herbs and spices steeped in a spirit. It is aged in oak vats.

Traditional leaders in food and drink, the French have their own favorite aperitifs. Among the most famous are Pernod, Ricard, Lillet and Dubonnet. Sweet anise-flavored aperitifs, Pernod and Ricard are descendants of Absinthe, the potent nineteenth-century "pastis" that was eventually outlawed. Poured over ice and water, they become cloudy.

A subtle aperitif with a hint of orange, Lillet comes from south of Bordeaux. The base wine is

ABSOLUT BRAVO.

infused with herbs and other botanicals, then adjusted for sweetness.

Dubonnet is another popular French aperitif. Available in Blanc and Rouge, it is sweet and aromatic and, like vermouth, made with an infusion of botanicals in a base wine. In fact, if Dubonnet is not available, a blend of equal parts of white and red vermouth makes a satisfactory substitute.

From England comes Pimm's No. 1 Cup. It has a gin base to which are added liqueurs, herbs and citrus extracts. Produced in London, Pimm's is usually served over ice with soda or tonic.

Another popular aperitif is Schnapps, the German name for aquavit. Aquavit is a dry spirit made from grains or potatoes and flavored with caraway seed.

On its own, plain Schnapps is not that popular in the United States. The American taste runs more to Schnapps with such enticing flavors as Peach Basket, Strawberry Patch, Piña Colada, Raspberry Ridge or Old Style Rootbeer. Schnapps can also be flavored with peppermint, apricot, pear, apple and blackberry. Flavored Schnapps are produced by Leroux, DeKuyper, Hiram Walker and Bols.

Finally, there is Moet & Chandon's Petite Liqueur, a delightful blend of aged Champagne and Cognac. Packaged in a miniature Champagne bottle complete with a cork, it is a sweet, slightly sparkling liqueur with a complex, mellow flavor of caramel. Petite Liqueur is best enjoyed chilled and served straight up, as an aperitif or an after-dinner drink. ▌

BRANDY

MOST SPIRITS CALLED BRANDY are distilled from grape wine, but there are also brandies made from various kinds of fruit like cherries, apples and plums. Eaux-de-vie, distilled fruit spirits, are often classified as brandies, but for the purist, only a brandy distilled from grapes merits the name.

COGNAC

"ALL COGNAC IS BRANDY, but not all brandy is Cognac," is an axiom with a specific point — there are a lot of brandies, but only those grown in the Cognac region of France may be called Cognac. The Cognac region is in west central France near the Atlantic Ocean, just north of Bordeaux. Of its six subregions, the best are Grande Champagne and Petite Champagne. Cognac is a blend of brandies, often coming from several of the subregions; a Fine Champagne is a blend of Grande Champagne and Petite Champagne brandies.

Cognac is distilled twice in a pot still and aged, first in new oak casks, then in older ones. Very old

Cognac is often moved into glass demijohns to prevent bitterness resulting from prolonged wood aging.

A Cognac must be aged in wood for at least two years before it is exported to the United States. A three-star Cognac is one aged a minimum of three years. The three-year minimum also applies to V.S. (Very Special). V.S.O.P. (Very Special Old Pale) and V.O. (Very Old) must be aged at least four years. Napoleon Grande Reserve, Paradis and Extra Vieille require a six-year minimum, though most are aged in wood much longer. Once bottled, Cognacs do not age further. Courvoisier, Hennessy and Martell are the major distillers of Cognac, but there are others offering a range of premium Cognacs. These include Hine, Delamain, Otard, Camus, Remy Martin and Salignac. Since many distillers prefer their own premium terms, Napoleon Cognacs, such as Courvoisier Napoleon, are often not labeled that way. Martell's Cordon Bleu, Hennessy's Bras d'Or and Polignac's Reserve Prince Hubert are popular examples.

Luxury Cognacs, often special lots from the dis-

If You're Lucky It Will Land On Your Arm.

SECTUR

RAVITS WATCHES & CLOCKS
San Francisco
(415) 392-1947

ANYTIME JEWELERS
Seattle
(206) 392-1981

tillery's private collection or *paradis,* are well-aged mellow spirits with great depth of flavor, often lavishly packaged in beautiful cut-crystal decanters. Among the best luxury Cognacs are Remy Martin Louis XIII Grand Fine and Remy Martin X.O., Hennessy X.O. Baccarat and Hennessy Paradis, Martell Reserve du Fondateur, Hine Triomphe, Courvoisier V.O.C. Fine Champagne and Delamain Daum Crystal.

ARMAGNAC

BECAUSE ARMAGNAC IS A SMALL, landlocked rural region, its excellent spirit is not as well known as Cognac. Located south of Bordeaux, Armagnac produces less brandy than Cognac does. Armagnac is distilled once in a small continuous still, which generates a higher concentration of flavor compo-

nents than does a pot still distillation. This gives Armagnac its characteristic flavor.

Armagnac has an aging system similar to that of Cognac. The minimum is eighteen months in oak, with V.O., V.S.O.P. and Reserve requiring a minimum of four years, while Hors d'Age, Napoleon, Extra and Vieille Reserve must be aged at least five.

With both Cognac and Armagnac, the law requires only a minimum aging. Thus a V.S.O.P., the most popular type, may in fact contain brandies much older than the required minimum of four years. Unlike Cognac, however, Armagnac does have vintage-dated bottles as well as brandies. Many distillers date the label with the year the spirit was made as well as the year it was bottled. Premium brands include Sempe, Samalens, Janneau, Larresingle, Marquis de Montesquiou, Marquis de Cassuade and De Montal.

LIQUEURS

IN THE SALONS of nineteenth-century England and Europe, it was common to serve a mild digestive to settle the stomach after a long, multi-course meal. The origin of liqueurs, however, can be traced to the sixteenth century when the liqueur Danzig Goldwasser first appeared. Made from exotic blends of herbs, barks and seeds, the first liqueurs were valued for their medicinal properties, although these were more imaginary than real.

In simple terms, a liqueur is a sweetened spirit base (a natural grain alcohol or grape *eau-de-vie*) flavored with a natural plant agent. The production of liqueurs is complicated and time consuming, often involving many steps and requiring expensive and scarce raw materials. There are two basic methods: maceration and distillation. Maceration is the simplest, soaking the flavoring substances in the spirit base until the alcohol is infused with their flavors.

Distillation is usually reserved for plants and herbs. The aim is not to produce flavored alcohol,

but to collect aromatic vapors and condense them into a liquid. The process often requires successive distillations to extract the essential oils of the raw material. After distillation or maceration, the liqueur is sweetened with a simple sugar syrup or sometimes honey. Water or neutral spirits are also added to adjust the alcohol content to between 25 and 40 percent. Finally, coloring, obtained from either certified food colors or an infusion of plants and fruits, is added to many liqueurs.

HERBAL LIQUEURS

IN THE MIDDLE AGES, certain plants, herbs and spices were used by alchemists for their medicinal properties. From these crude medicines, liqueurs were created. Many of the classic herbal liqueurs, such as Benedictine and Chartreuse, were made in monasteries as curatives.

Benedictine, originally made by Benedictine

monks, is thought to date from 1510, which makes it one of the oldest liqueurs. Benedictine production was placed in secular hands in 1863, where it remains today. A proprietary blend of twenty-seven ingredients, it is dark amber in color, medium sweet, with a soft flavor like vanilla, almond and honey. In 1938, Benedictine created B&B, a blend of the liqueur and aged Cognac, which is drier and more like brandy.

Chartreuse is made in two styles: the original green, lightly sweet with a complex spicy-peppery flavor, and the sweeter, lower alcohol yellow. Both green and yellow are also available in a limited V.E.P. (aged for twelve years) bottling.

Other popular liqueurs include the Basque Izarra, the German Jaegermeister, and the Italian Liquore Galliano made from anise and herbs.

PLANT & SEED LIQUEURS

ALSO KNOWN FOR THEIR RESTORATIVE properties, seed and plant liqueurs differ in that they are often flavored by just one substance, such as aniseed, mint, caraway or coffee.

The list of plant and seed liqueurs is lengthy. Among the best known are Anisette, made from aniseed, not licorice; Crème de Menthe, made from mint leaves in both clear and green styles; Crème de Cacao, made from vanilla pods and cocoa beans; Vandermint, made from mint and chocolate; Kahlua, a Mexican liqueur made from coffee, with a chocolate-like flavor; and Amaretto di Saronno, made not from almonds but from crushed apricot pits.

Others include Sambuca Romana, made from the elder flower, which is similar in character to aniseed; Kummel, made from caraway or cumin seeds; Truffles chocolate liqueur and Marie Brizard's Chocolat; Cheri-Suisse, with a chocolate-cherry flavor; Tia Maria, a Jamaican coffee liqueur; Peachtree Schnapps, with a natural peach flavor; Frangelico, made from hazelnuts; and Crème de Noyaux, similar to Amaretto since it is made from apricot or peach pits.

FRUIT LIQUEURS

SINCE CAPTURING A TRUE FRUIT FLAVOR is often an elusive exercise, fruit liqueurs are perhaps the most difficult to make.

The most common fruit liqueurs are made from oranges. Grand Marnier, based on Cognac and the essence of Caribbean bitter orange, is one of the best known. Grand Marnier Cordon Rouge is a blend of three-to-five-year-old Cognac and distilled orange liqueur. It is matured in large oak uprights for nine to twelve months before bottling.

Another well-known French liqueur is Cointreau, produced from the peels of bitter and sweet oranges. Mandarine Napoleon, from Belgium, is similar to Grand Marnier but has a distinctive tangerine and herb flavor. Curaçao, Triple Sec and Spain's Liquor Gran Torres are other notable orange liqueurs.

Second in number only to citrus-flavored liqueurs are those made from cherries. The best-known are Peter Heering from Denmark and Cherry Marnier from France.

The flavor cornucopia of fruit liqueurs also includes raspberry, blackberry, strawberry, banana, apricot and peach (Pêcher Mignon is made from white peaches). Exotic fruit liqueurs such as La Grande Passion, made of passionfruit, and Midori, made in Japan from melons, have also made a splash. Cassis, a black currant drink, is actually too low in alcohol for legitimate standing as a liqueur.

BRANDY & WHISKEY LIQUEURS

THIS SPECIALTY GROUP differs in that the producer adds a bit of grape brandy or grain whiskey to flavor an otherwise bland high-proof spirit.

Grand Marnier, also noted earlier as a fruit liqueur, is the premier brandy-based liqueur. Besides Cordon Rouge, Grand Marnier produces Cherry Marnier and a special Cuvée du Centenaire. Other popular brandy liqueurs include Metaxa from Greece and the lesser-known Italian Tuaca.

Popular Scottish liqueurs include Drambuie, a blend of Scotch whiskey, herbs and honey, and the less intense Lochan Ora. Irish Mist, also based on a recipe of herbs and honey, is lighter and drier. The best-known American whiskey liqueur is Southern Comfort, with a sweet peachy flavor and subtle citrus notes. ☗

Gerald D. Boyd is a widely published wine and spirits writer based in San Francisco.

Epicurean Rendezvous

gratefully acknowledges the support
of the following sponsors

RESTAURANT INDEX

CUISINE KEY

AMR = American	ITA = Italian
CAL = California	JPN = Japanese
CHI = Chinese	MED = Mediterranean
CON = Continental	MEX = Mexican
CRE = Creole/Cajun	ORI = Oriental
EUR = European	
FRN = French	STK = Steakhouse
INT = International	TRO = Tropical